Assessment in the multi-ethnic primary classroom

edited by Pat Keel

tb

Trentham Books

First published in 1994 by Trentham Books Limited

Trentham Books Limited
Westview House
734 London Road
Oakhill
Stoke-on-Trent
Staffordshire
England ST4 5NP

© Pat Keel 1994

British Cataloguing in Publication Data
A catalogue record for this book is available from the British Library.

ISBN: 0 948080 51 5

Cover designed by Shawn Stipling.

Designed and typeset by Trentham Print Design Limited, Chester and
printed in Great Britain by Bemrose Shafron Limited, Chester

iv

Assessment in the multi-ethnic
primary classroom

Contents

Acknowledgements

The publishers called this book a 'weepie', because it was so long and difficult in the making — but neither the authors nor the publishers could prevent the National Curriculum assessment arrangements also being long and difficult in the making. At different stages we waited for the picture to clarify, and we are still waiting. However it became clear that the principles upon which we began writing have remained valid and continue to apply.

We and the publishers, especially Gillian Klein, worked closely throughout. Thanks are owed to everyone who contributed for their efforts and patience. Numerous other people, colleagues and, not least, our families, gave their time and support of all kinds — the book could not have been written without them!

Abbreviations

AT	Attainment Target
CLPE	Centre for Language in Primary Education
CRE	Commission for Racial Equality
CUES	Centre for Urban Educational Studies
DES	Department of Education and Science
DFE	Department for Education
EC	European Commission
EFL	English as a foreign language
ESL	English as a second language
GM	Grant Maintained
IDP	Institutional Development Plan
ILEA	Inner London Education Authority
INSET	In-service educational training
LEA	Local Education Authority
LINC	Language in the National Curriculum
LMS	Local Management of Schools
NALDIC	National Association for Language Development in the Curriculum
NATE	National Association for the Teaching of English
NCC	National Curriculum Council
NCP	New Commonwealth Pupil
NFER	National Foundation for Educational Research
NUT	National Union of Teachers
OFSTED	Office for Standards in Education
PACT	Parents and children and teachers
PLR	Primary Language Record
PoS	Programmes of Study
RoA	Record of Achievement
QTS	Qualified teacher status
SATs	Standard Assessment Tasks
SCAA	Schools Curriculum Assessment Authority
SEAC	School Examinations and Assessment Council
SEN	Special Educational Needs
SoA	Statement of Attainment [now Level Description]
SRB	Single Regeneration Budget
TESOL	Teaching English to speakers of other languages
TGAT	Task Group on Assessment and Testing
UK	United Kingdom

Notes on Contributors

Pauline Lyseight-jones has worked in primary, secondary, further and higher education and in the voluntary education sector. She has contributed to several books and journals. Currently she is General Inspector for Curriculum Evaluation and assessment in the London Borough of Ealing.

Updesh Porter has taught in East Africa and in the UK. She has been involved in second language acquisition and community language teaching and is currently a senior co-ordinator for Section 11 in Ealing.

Celia Burgess-Macey is an early years and primary adviser in Lambeth Education Department and began her career as a child care officer. She contributed to the Rampton inquiry, worked as a tutor at CUES, and lectured at Anglia Polytechnic. She is joining the Early Years research team at the Institute of Education.

Martin Francis is deputy headteacher in a Brent primary school, responsible for pastoral care, parental links and SEN. As a member of ALTARF [All London Teachers Against Racism and Facism] he contributed to *Challenging Racism* [1984], the ALTARF *Newsletter* and *Issues in Race and Education.*

Elaine Sturman is an advisory teacher for assessment in Ealing and has teaching experience at both primary and secondary levels. She worked at CUES, and contributed to the ALTARF *Newsletter* and *Issues in Race and Education* and co-edited *Bilingual Learners in Secondary Schools.*

Maggie Gravelle has taught in inner-city primary and secondary schools for over 25 years and has wide experience of INSET. She runs a Section 11 funded project in Lewisham and is about to take up a post a Greenwich University. She has published articles in several journals including *Issues in Race and Education.*

Patsy Daniels has been a school governor and clerk to governors for several years. A mother of school-age children, including foster children, she works as an administrative officer with the National Curriculum Assessment Team in a London LEA.

Rehana Minhas is a General Inspector with Haringey LEA with a brief for Equal Opportunities and was Director of the Community Division of CUES. She chaired the Public Inquiry into the Recruitment and Promotion of Ethnic Minority Teachers in Ealing, *Ealing's Dilemma*. She is co-author of *Equal Opportunities in the New Era* and a founder member of CARE, the Campaign for Anti-Racist Education.

Pat Keel's teaching experience since 1960 has been across phases — in Singapore, Malaysia, Indonesia and UK. Her fields are language development, equal opportunities in education and action research in the classroom. She has published articles on these subjects. She currently runs the Section 11 project for schools and colleges in Greenwich.

Introduction

Assessment in the multi-ethnic primary classroom

Reason for assessment (handwritten annotation)

A major effect of the 1988 Education Reform Act has been to bring assessment to centre stage in education. The Act was introduced as part of a range of reforms by a Conservative government anxious to fulfil several linked political agendas. These included releasing free enterprise and competition into traditionally public-service areas like education and health, previously kept relatively safe from the harsh vagaries of the economic market place. So doing, they claimed, would provide accountability and choice to the consumer. By contrast with this apparent devolution of institutional power to individuals through free enterprise, there has been a determined drive to wrest power from local government and invest it in centrally appointed quangos. In education, local management of schools and colleges is one side of this coin, and the National Curriculum and its assessment the other.

politics (handwritten annotation)

Although the range of public examinations in this country has steadily increased over the past fifty years (Gipps, 1990), the government's wish to publish national assessment results at Key Stages of the National Curriculum in league tables as part of the drive to generate competition, choice and accountability, has impelled the machinery of public examinations into all primary and secondary classrooms. Every teacher is now responsible for assessing pupils' achievement against National Curriculum Attainment Targets and their Level Descriptions, and for preparing pupils for Standard Assessment Tasks, or national tests at the end of Key Stages. As Sutton (1992) observes, this responsibility is crucial and teachers need, more than ever before, to be clear about what constitutes effective school-based assessment.

When implementation of this programme of assessment began in schools fundamental difficulties soon emerged and generated growing criticism among teachers. Basic tensions and contradictions within the perceived purposes, both educational and political, of the assessment programme, have surfaced over the years of attempted implementation. As a result, the government had to take a step back, in response to sustained objections and widespread refusal by teachers to carry out the assessment programme in summer 1993. Sir Ron Dearing was appointed to review the National Curriculum and its assessment. The government said that they would allow more opportunity for debate and time for change. Teachers hoped that a programme of assessment might be formulated which had clearly useful purposes and which could be delivered logistically.

As the National Curriculum assessments came further on stream from 1990 onwards, a host of questions were raised over their purposes, practicality, reliability and validity, as well as their fairness, especially in the context of pupils with less favourable chances of achieving good performance and results in these assessments. However, overarching all this, there is the question of core concern for teachers: how best to manage the assessment of each pupil's progress within the framework of what is statutorily required.

This book focuses on assessment specifically in relation to pupils from ethnic minority backgrounds — as opposed to those of the indigenous or ethnic majority. Since the 1960s pupils with origins in the British New Common-wealth countries have represented the largest identifiable group of black and bilingual pupils in our schools. However, the authors here make reference also to more recently arrived pupils, most of whom are likely to be members of families resident in Britain as refugees from African and Middle Eastern states. The impact on our schools of children who have come as the result of the break-up of Yugoslavia is yet to be determined.

The National Curriculum and its assessment are likely to impinge in significantly different ways on this group of pupils, compared to their indigenous peers, because of their particular linguistic or cultural backgrounds and because of their often negative reception in this country. In this book we refer to these pupils as black, the term 'black' being not necessarily a description of colour but signifying the commonalities of background and experience just described. The rationale for treating them as a group has largely to do with the 'host' community's perceptions of and behaviour towards them. In fact black minorities are the opposite of a homogeneous group — rather absurdly, the term 'ethnic' is frequently used to refer solely to them and their cultures.

Over the past three decades, much research (including that for the government Committee of Inquiry first set up in 1978 and reporting finally under Lord Swann in 1985], was predicated on — and in turn confirmed — the educational 'underachievement' of black pupils, taken as a group. Yet over the past decade it has been shown that some groups of black pupils are high achievers. There has been corresponding evidence to show also that pupils from lower socio-economic classes, and pupils with special educational needs, whatever their ethnic group, also achieve at lower than average levels. Gender can be a factor in achievement too. Girls achieve better than boys in language for example, but boys do better in science. Recent signs indicate that black girls achieve better terminal exam results than black boys.

'Under-achievement' is therefore relative in all groups. Moreover, some of the operative disadvantages and some of the strategies that might be used to overcome or at least reduce them, often apply across these categories of pupils. For example, when equal opportunities policies are applied effectively in an institution, this is likely to reduce disadvantage for all groups.

Thus, although the book addresses the assessment and achievement of black and bilingual pupils, so considered in the context of the multi-ethnic classroom, the authors would argue that most issues considered here have relevance in any classroom in Britain. Furthermore, despite the fact that there are some places with no black settlement as yet, one does not have far to travel to reach well-established settlements of numerous ethnic minority groups in all our main conurbations. The UK today cannot be seen as anything but multi-ethnic and multicultural. Inextricable historical links with other countries, including those with past colonies, upon which Britain must build for the future, make it imperative to educate all children to function within a multi-ethnic, multicultural framework. The issues in this book have relevance beyond Britain. We have in mind all countries where there are dominant eurocentric cultures, alongside which cultures of minority groups should take their rightful place.

This book is a collection of independent contributions by people who are involved in the day to day delivery of education in schools — as teachers, advisory teachers, inspectors or officers. They do not attempt to write academically — their views, based on their practical experience, are presented to similar practitioners, to parents and governors. Their jobs, as for most people in education, have in recent years become demanding to an often nonsensical degree. They nevertheless believed that writing the chapters of book was worth the effort.

The first chapter offers a nut-shell overview of the position of black pupils in this country, dating from the 1960s when their arrival first impacted significantly on schools. It is argued that the previously-held assumptions and responses in education to their languages and cultural backgrounds continue essentially to inform official policies thirty years on.

In Chapter 2 Pauline Lyseight-jones illustrates through several parables how some mistaken but common assumptions can dangerously underlie intentions and expectations in education, and likewise in assessment. We are suitably warned of the inexactness of any system of assessment. She, like other authors here, stresses the prime importance of addressing the individual learning needs of every child, regardless of ethnic background, gender, ability, etc through progressive diagnostic and informative assessment.

Several inter-linked issues to do with language are still to be resolved within the National Curriculum and Assessment. Some are related to English as a subject. There is much disquiet over the present English Orders, eg over the narrowness of prescribed texts for literature. There is also dissatisfaction over the prescription of a restricted 'Standard English' and 'grammar'. Linked with these issues is a wider one — the approaches in the curriculum to languages other than English.

None of these issues are new. They have remained largely unresolved since even before the sixties, when they became highlighted by the arrival of New Commonwealth pupils. Absolutely fundamental to the education of these pupils is the perceived relationship between the English language and other languages. Blinkered monolingualism is virtually a national characteristic. Success in learning other languages has been dismal, compared with what people in other countries world-wide achieve. There is a reluctance to state publicly that a repertoire of languages would be of economic benefit. In education there is scant recognition of the cognitive advantages of bilingual competence that is suggested by research. Chapter 3 focuses on a major issue underlying the chances of achievement for many black children, ie their development of their first language. It is argued by Updesh Porter and Pat Keel that policies on language are somewhat inconsistent.

Under-fives education is in the spotlight, as the government acknowledges the sound sense of investing in the proven benefits of good nursery schooling. However this has become another political issue. The report of the Paul Hamlyn Foundation National Commission for Education [1993] and more recently, *Start Right: The Importance of Early Learning* [RSA, 1994], a study by an advisory committee led by Sir Christopher Ball, both recommended universal quality provision for under-fives, and both suggested ways of funding it. The government would like to achieve improved provision by supporting the many private playgroups and nurseries that have mushroomed in response to demand. But such provision may not be universally accessible to all children, nor necessarily all of high quality.

In Chapter 4 Celia Burgess-Macey takes up the educational issues at the core of the debate on the assessment of young children. She emphasises the necessity of adopting assessment systems which do not restrict individual children's early development by focusing narrowly on preparation for the National Curriculum. She stresses the need for an assessment practice built on an understanding of young children's learning and compatible with an early years' curriculum based on the same principles.

Maggie Gravelle and Elaine Sturman, in Chapter 5 analyse the 1993/4 Key Stage 1 Assessment Folder, indicating that SEAC and later SCAA made some progress in acknowledging the presence of bilingual children and the need to take account of their first languages. They also reveal dangerous assumptions of deficit that are made about bilingual learners. The issues they raise in relation to the School Assessment Folder have implications for all Key Stages.

Elaine Sturman and Martin Francis consider, in Chapter 6, teachers' unease with the strictures imposed on the primary curriculum by the National Curriculum and assessment system expected by the government. They highlight the essentials of a motivating curriculum for pupils, which should include continuous assessment.

The 1988 Education Reform Act placed unprecedented legal responsibility on parents for shaping how their child's school delivers education within the framework of the National Curriculum. In Chapter 7 Patsy Daniels explains many of the challenges that black parents face in taking up this duty.

One institution within the education system which could speedily bring about beneficial change for black children's education is OFSTED. The Framework for Inspections has made a significant contribution, regaining some of the ground lost for equal opportunities in the context of the National Curriculum and the politics of the Education Reform Act. In Chapter 8 Rehana Minhas shows how issues to do with improving the standards of these pupils' education and achievement fit into the framework for Inspections of schools. She discusses the potential influence of OFSTED since its beginnings this decade, particularly if it overcomes some of its weaknesses.

Ostensibly, Section 11 funding was aimed at supporting black children's access to achievement in education, but has it achieved this? The final chapter covers the saga of this resource — its tragic past failures, and its tenuous successes, which may now be stunted by a radical reform of resourcing looming on the horizon.

The past five years have been painful for teachers. They have had to face unprecedented criticism from a government which has needed toe-holds — and scapegoats — in progressing its political and economic agendas, often on the back of education. Teachers have been trapped in silent acquiescence by hurriedly passed bills which swept in massive demands upon their profession. They were hardly consulted, and in any case not listened to or respected for their own working experience. Constructive dialogue would far sooner have brought us all nearer to the prize of a National Curriculum and assessment system which we could all proudly own. But ownership has had to be fought for by teachers, and that struggle has cost valuable time and goodwill.

The government may yet come to recognise that formulating a National Curriculum and its assessment will take years of hard, dedicated and co-operative effort by all interested parties — the government, teachers, parents, employers and, most importantly, the children whose futures it will shape. This book is intended to be a contribution to the essential debate. That debate must address how the curriculum and assessment can help to shape a multi-ethnic, multilingual and pluralistic society, all sections of which share equitably in the outcomes of a good education.

Chapter 1

Beginnings of the
multi-ethnic classroom

Pat Keel

We are over here because you were over there.
— (Sivanandan quoted in Moore, 1975)

It is salutory to bear in mind the factors that brought black pupils into British classrooms. We know that there have been Africans in Britain since at least Roman times (Fryer, 1984). Their presence is documented from Elizabethan times (e.g. File and Power, 1981). There are communities established since the nineteenth century in seaports such as Liverpool, Cardiff and Bristol, whose forebears were seamen of African, Asian and Chinese origin. Those seamen, along with countless other black people, over the long history of slavery and then colonialism and its irrevocable aftermath, contributed and still contribute abundantly to the wealth and relatively raised standards of living in Europe. Despite such vital involvement between Britain and its colonies, today the black population here is less than 6%, about half of whom are British-born.

The Museum of London recently held an exhibition called *The Peopling of London: overseas communities from BC to 1993*. A range of documents and artefacts showed the historical contexts relating to the lives of black people of various backgrounds in this country. The exhibition and events around it, which drew together different London communities in sharing their experiences, have provided pupils and teachers with invaluable material directly relevant to the National Curriculum. For teachers especially, this exhibition offered an opportunity to fill significant gaps in background awareness essential for any modem teacher, yet often sadly lacking in teacher training programmes.

50s-60s Immigration

Returning to the pupils with whom we are particularly concerned in this book, their first entry in significant numbers began in the 1960s during the post-war industrial boom. To alleviate the shortage of workers for factories in major industrial areas, the national health service and city transport systems, the government turned to its colonies in Asia and the Caribbean (i.e. New Commonwealth countries) and campaigned there for people to come and work in Britain.

In South Asia national and state boundaries drawn during the last days of the British Raj in 1947 were a key factor in setting off waves of migration within the region and to other countries, including Britain. The economic depression after the war in the Caribbean, due partly to a world-wide fall in the prices of export crops developed under colonialism, also made it necessary for people to leave their homes in the sun for the harsher climates of the United States and Europe (Moore, 1975, Fryer, 1984, Carter, 1986). In 1952 the United States restricted immigration from, among other areas, the West Indies. However, Asians and West Indians in British colonies had British passports and the 1948 Nationality Act gave them citizenship of the United Kingdom and the right to come to live here permanently. Several thousand came in search of work and economic stability. Their experience of a colonial education had engendered notions of belonging and loyalty to the 'mother country', but their subsequent disillusionment on arrival here is well documented (e.g. Wilson, 1978; Sivanandan, 1982; Rushdie, 1982; Carter, 1986).

Discrimination and disillusionment

Apart from their shock at coming face to face with sheer racial bigotry at street level, they were often disillusioned over the low status work they were offered, regardless of the skills and experience with which so many of them had come (Fryer, op. cit). The fact that post-war economic development in Europe and the United States has been based largely on the exploitation of low paid, low status immigrant workers, often kept without citizenship by regulations, is generally ignored (Moore, op. cit). That exploitation continues, ironically hand in hand with exaggerated paranoia across Europe about being invaded by illegal immigrants and the need to protect European frontiers against these imagined hordes.

The popular media have always tended to whip up latent anti-black prejudice, especially in times of economic down-turn. Black people living in this country become a convenient scapegoat in the simple mind, for the causes of unemployment, lack of housing or reported increase in crime. Bankrupt politicians often appeal to such popular notions when electioneering. Neo-nazis base their appeal on the same messages — 'they take our jobs, houses and social benefit'. This appeal to the emotions has won bye-elections in the '70s (Smethick) and helped win national elections, e.g. Thatcher's 1979 speech expressing the fear that 'our culture' (never explained) is being 'swamped'. In September, 1993 a candidate from the largest English fascist party (BNP) won a bye-election in Millwall, in London's east end, a significantly impoverished and traditionally immigrant area with a high level of unemployment. The mythology remains unchallenged — few are interested in the facts. When the facts are examined — and they probably never have been in the popular media — statistics on unemployment, housing, social services and education show, survey upon survey, that black people as a group are disproportionately disadvantaged (Brown, 1984; Amin, 1992).

That British institutions, like society in general, respond negatively to black people would seem a large factor in explaining this disadvantage, admitted in major inquiries such as Scarman (1981) and Swann (1985). Although net emigration from Britain has consistently been higher than net immigration over the past 25 years — with the exception of one year (Twitchin, 1988) — immigration law and policies have been systematically tightened against black people. They continue to face often grossly unfair immigration procedures, even as visitors. The media and politicians constantly exploit the immigration of black people as representing a dangerous 'swamping' of the country, when no statistics exist to support the claim.

The UK has not conducted empirical research into the actual social and economic effects that immigrants have on the country of settlement. In Germany there is an extensive programme of research, looking at the impact of Turkish *Gastwerkers* and the East German *Ausländers* in particular. The evidence points to a substantial net gain to the host country. Immigrants use less than the indigenous population of the resources devoted to health care and social care and with their labour and industry contribute disproportionately highly to the wealth of their host country (Spencer, 1994).

It is no wonder in the face of pervasive negativity to black people, that the Race Relations Acts of 1965, 1967, 1968 and 1976 had little in the way of a will to make them effective. Rather, experience over the years since they were put into place, has demonstrated their inadequacy in bringing individual cases of racial discrimination to court, and of getting redress. However, they have served as a tool in bringing about the adoption of equal opportunities policies in various institutions including LEAs, although it is said that these policies are often mere pieces of paper, filed and forgotten (Richardson, 1983; Troyna and Ball, 1983; Macdonald et al, 1989).

The Commission for Racial Equality (CRE) has successfully supported a number of cases where racial discrimination has been proved, thus establishing important precedents, notably in employment practice, and some in education, mentioned later in Chapter 9. Nevertheless, the number of proven cases remains dismally low, compared to the number of complaints received (Klein, 1993). Much work is needed to extend the use of the law as it stands, and to demonstrate its present weakness and lobby for its strengthening. In March 1994 a private member's bill successfully removed an upper limit (previously £2,000.00) for fines for proven racial discrimination.

In recent years vicious racial attacks have escalated dramatically, while neo-nazis are gaining support across Europe. The Runneymede Trust tracks race issues — policies, policing, immigration, harassment, etc — in Britain and European countries. Their monthly bulletin indicates that manifestations of racism have steadily increased. Part of this trend has been the lack of government action to counter racism at any level. Black staff in some legal departments in local authorities have begun to set out procedures for workers in housing, social services departments and education for dealing with complaints of racial attacks or harassment. These procedures ensure that information, which can facilitate charges being brought to court, is elicited and recorded when a complaint is first made. However, it may be that the EC will lead more pertinently on law against racial discrimination and violence.

Within the last decade we have witnessed repeated legislation resulting in major social reform, e.g. new laws relating to tax, trade unions, health, housing, welfare, policing, penal and judical systems. We are yet to work out the full implications of such legislation in terms of racial justice, or at least in relation to the Race Relation Acts. This was illustrated in the context of the 1988 Education Reform Act, where a parent's right to choose, in this case to remove her child from a school on racial grounds, was upheld first by the Secretary of State for Education, and then in the courts (Hillcole Group, 1991, Troyna and Hatcher, 1992).

Responses in Education

A further cause of disillusionment for black settlers of the 1950s and 60s from South Asia and the Caribbean was the education of their children. They had learnt to place importance on education as a means of improving prospects for better paid and higher status jobs. Their generally low job status in this country led them to base their hopes on their children's education. This would be the means by which their children, if not they themselves, would be fulfilled in status and economic well-being. Running parallel with this expectation was their faith and trust in the UK education system. In their countries of origin, teachers were respected and trusted with the task of educating the children. As a rule parents did not interfere with the school. They could assume that their responsibility lay in taking care of their children at home. By the mid 1970s, they realised that in Britain it was significantly otherwise, and that they would have to intervene to prevent neglect or mismanagement of their children's education within the system (Coard, 1971; Carter, 1986).

The first government response in education to the arrival of children new to English in schools was based on the belief that they should be taught English as quickly as possible and be assimilated into English culture. Teachers were assigned the task of teaching these children English in separate units either in the school or off-site. The emphasis was on teaching them English until they knew enough to join the mainstream curriculum. It was assumed that Caribbean children were not new to English and they were expected to cope in the British classroom. They after all did not have the 'language problems' of their Asian counterparts. The latter group were described by some educationists as 'non-English speakers'. More recently, they have been named more positively as 'bilinguals' or 'emerging bilinguals'.

Bussing

In 1965 the Department for Education and Science (DES), without consulting black parents, allowed LEAs to practice 'bussing' or dispersal of black children from their local schools, wherever they might otherwise form over a third of the roll, to spread them across other schools. The reason offered was that dispersal would be good for these children educationally, assist assimilation, and even benefit the majority cultures. It is significant that no white children were subjected to the inconvenience (Klein, 1993). Black children spent time and energy on travel and were more vulnerable out of their area to racial harassment (Dhondy *et al*, 1982). The somewhat contradictory rationale only thinly disguised a more pressing need to assuage the complaints coming from white parents. They believed that the presence of black pupils was disadvantaging their children in diverting too much teacher attention. Troyna and Williams (1986) have shown how the state, in failing to acknowledge underlying racism, has constantly been at odds with itself in making coherent policy in relation to the presence of black children.

Provision for English Language teaching

In 1966 the government responded in Section 11 of the Local Government Act to complaints from local authorities about their financial burdens caused by servicing the needs of large numbers of 'immigrants' from the New Commonwealth. This legislation provided local authorities with extra funds paid through the Home Office, based on numbers settled within the authority, for services in housing, social services and education. The bulk of funding has always gone to education. The fund paid 75% towards the salary costs of staff employed 'in addition' to mainstream staff, to service the 'special needs' of those of New Commonwealth origin 'whose language or customs differ from the rest of the community' (Home Office). Schools with numbers of New Commonwealth children were allocated staff whose salaries were 75% Home Office funded. Teachers who provided the children with English language support were usually paid for in this way, and for many of them teaching English as a Second Language (ESL) became their career (See Chapters 3 and 9).

Children new to English could spend extensive periods in an English language support unit, to all intents and purposes being immersed in 'second language' English, but missing out meanwhile on the mainstream curriculum. Texts used then show the inadequacy of 'second language' English teaching, particularly in its stilted usage and lack of practical context. Line drawings of objects illustrated sentences like 'This is a house'. Children remained isolated from their indigenous peers and therefore unable to pick up the real language of communication in the classroom and playground. They could fall significantly behind their peers in the rest of the curriculum, and by the mid 70s it was evident that there was serious cause for concern regarding the achievement levels of black pupils.

It is worth recalling that the Bullock Report (1975) had at that time argued for the necessity to recognise a child's home language and culture, and to reflect these in the curriculum. Bullock also stressed that every teacher, through the medium of their subject, uses language, and therefore has significant opportunities for teaching language while transmitting particular subject knowledge. The advice seems to have fallen on deaf ears. There was no sign of it being taken up in teacher training. In schools, there was generally complete disregard for the children's home language or cultural background. These were seen as irrelevant at best — at worst, home languages were seen as impediments to progress in learning English and assimilating into English culture. Use of home languages at school was frowned upon by teachers, and they often advised families preferably not to speak it at home either. Many Asians will confirm this experience. There were numerous instances of closed minds towards accommodating home cultures within the context of the school. For example, Sikh boys often faced objections to their turbans, and cases of dispute persisted into recent years (CRE, 1991) over such matters as girls not being permitted to wear *hijab* (headscarf) or *shalwar kameez*; a Rastafarian asked to cut his hair 'properly'.

The Caribbean child, on the other hand, although bussed along with Asian children, was perceived by teachers as one who should understand and use English as a first language and therefore as not eligible for English language support. That the child often appeared not to correspond with this expectation was probably struck teachers as perversity. It is only with the last decade that there has been a growing realisation that Caribbean children also bring with them background languages or at least other varieties of English. Linguistic studies of Creoles have led to their acceptance as separate language systems. A lack of awareness of such realities, coupled with the presence of historically rooted racial prejudice, contributed to Caribbean pupils coming to be placed with excessive frequency during the 60s in lower attainment bands. They were also disproportionately diagnosed as 'educationally subnormal' and consigned to ESN schools, or units for children with learning and behavioural difficulties (Coard, 1971). One authority was prepared to admit that they were guilty of so discriminating against Caribbean origin boys (see Carter, 1986), but refused to do anything to put matters right for them.

'Underachievement'

By the 1970s, attention was being focused on the underachievement of black children. ILEA Research and Statistics Group surveys (1967) were showing lower levels of attainment for black as against indigenous children. The Newsom and Plowden Reports in the 60s had linked underachievement and lower socio-economic background but, during the 70s, black parents and teachers (see Maxwell, 1968; Coard, 1971; Stone, 1981) began identifying the ways that the education system was discriminating against their children. Black parent, student and community groups frequently protested in inner-city areas about issues such as bussing or dispersal, segregation in separate units, and about their overall dissatisfaction with the educational provision being offered to them and the relatively poor outcomes in terms of examinations and jobs.

They acted by organising their own alternative or support provision (Carter, 1986). In the Saturday or supplementary schools they set up, an atmosphere of strong identity, support and motivation provided some redress to pupils whose parents sent them there. Otherwise black pupils often faced a prospect of poor school-leaving certificates and job opportunities.

Black communities have over the years expressed their views of a system that by its ethnocentricity ignored the cultural and linguistic backgrounds of black pupils or even operated directly negative images and stereotypes (see also Chapter 7). Research suggested that black children had poor self-images (Milner, 1975). They preferred to have white friends, represented themselves as white in drawings, etc. These attitudes were seen to be the consequence of an ethnocentric education system and then strongly linked with their poor achievement (e.g. Bagley and Coard, 1975; Milner, 1975). This line of reasoning led to the ideology of the multicultural curriculum or differential curriculum for black pupils (e.g. Black Studies) aimed at positively representing black people and thereby building better self-images for black pupils. The rhetoric of the need for a multicultural curriculum for a multicultural society penetrated to documents from the Department of Education (e.g. DES, 1977), and is still in evidence today in patches of the National Curriculum. It can now, as it was then, be taken up in practice or ignored, depending on the persuasion of individual teachers, schools and LEAs.

Multicultural education
During the 1980s multicultural education was assumed by some white enthusiasts as the antidote to all the past deficiencies in the system. Many teachers, schools and some LEAs, backed by DES statements and some centrally provided INSET at the time, set about building positive images of black cultures and languages. Ethnic minority festivals were celebrated at school assemblies, grateful parents often providing the appropriate food, dress and music. 'Welcome' notices in various languages adorned school entrances, and one still sees displays of cultural artefacts. Unfortunately, those initiatives on their own could not tackle the problem at its roots.

Major publishers realised the market value and rushed in with a plethora of illustrations for at least the covers of books, which now might include a token black or brown face. However, the quality of new materials has improved over time. There are some excellent examples of books now, in terms of both themes and illustrations (See Klein, 1984,1985; Brooking, Foster and Smith, 1987). Nevertheless, school libraries may still have materials with negative bias or glaring omissions, often to the point of gross misinformation. There are, for instance, many distortions of fact in the histories of the Egyptians and other African civilisations.

Teacher Education

On the whole, core courses in teacher education have failed to reflect the learning needs of black and bilingual children, let alone address the pedagogic underpinnings of multicultural education, so that it might become acceptable as legitimate curriculum development (Jones and Street-Porter, 1989). Studies to support curriculum development along these lines (at first specifically to raise issues of race in the classroom) was led in the 70s by Lawrence Stenhouse in the Schools Council Humanities Project. But the materials produced were not acceptable to the DES, and this significant initiative in confronting racism was lost to policy development nationally (Stenhouse *et al*, 1982).

Thus without central government endorsement, there has been a situation in which so-called multicultural education initiatives become, as critics have suggested, bolted on, tokenistic, and pedagogically untested. Right-wing critics labelled multicultural education as a political bandwagon, and later used it as a target for attacking Labour-held LEAs, where such initiatives were being taken into schools. Other critics, both black and white, dismissed the initiatives as 'saris, somosas and steelbands', and exposed it as largely rhetoric which ignores core racism in the system (Troyna and Williams, 1986).

Identifying racism

Maureen Stone's (1981) research challenged the notion that black children necessarily suffer from poor self-image. She argues that in a society that is chronically racist, tinkering with the curriculum to make it suitable for black children is not going to change the society they have to face on leaving school. She believed it to be a myth that multicultural education would equip black children with the skills and certificates needed in the world of work. She advocated that teachers concentrate on formally teaching children essential knowledge, skills and abilities rather than assuming a role in therapies for improving self-concept. She pointed to the success of supplementary schools in providing basic knowledge and skills as worthy of emulation.

The government's responses in education from the late 1960s included various committee inquiries into the education of black pupils. The most significant of these was the government Committee of Inquiry chaired by Anthony Rampton. Black members of that committee insisted on identifying racism as a key factor for change in education (Carter, 1986). There had been a similar experience with the Scarman inquiry into the 1981 inner-city disturbances and that report eventually identified racism as a key factor. Both reports contributed to an important shift from seeing black cultures and languages as the problem, to recognising that the problem rested deep within white society's attitudinal and institutional racism. The struggle over achieving this shift saw the resignation of Rampton and several other members in the troubled years of the inquiry. Under Swann the final report, *Education for All*, emerged in 1985, with a mass of evidence pointing to the general underachievement of black and bilingual pupils, and the causes in the system for this failure, of which a major cause was the racism identified as permeating the system. The recommendations caused bitter disappointment in failing to endorse bilingual education as part of the curriculum needed for a culturally plural society, but it did strongly recommend that a curriculum that sought to challenge racism was appropriate for all pupils.

During the late 1980s, advocates for multicultural education argued for an underlying emphasis on challenging racism within curriculum development. Many teachers innovated in their classrooms and developed appropriate teaching materials, and literature appeared suggesting approaches in curriculum subjects (e.g. Craft and Klein, 1986; Gill and Levidow, 1987). This movement has continued to date. Materials have been produced inexpensively at LEA teacher centres (e.g. Birmingham, Coventry, Leicester, Bradford, Sheffield, Avon, Brent, Hounslow, and many others) but there is as yet no co-ordinated dissemination of these materials, produced in the first instance for use in local schools. Consequently, wide-spread use of some excellent classroom and school practice has been relatively slower than if there had been the will in the DES to support initiatives and co-ordinate dissemination. Also there has probably been some unnecessary duplication of effort in producing materials.

Meanwhile the publication of useful material in journals (e.g. *Multicultural Teaching, Issues in Race and Education*) has grown, and a number of useful books are now available to guide the subject teachers who are committed to principles of education for equal opportunities in a multiethnic society. The Runnymede Trust's *Teaching for Equality —Educational resources on race and gender,* by Brooking, Foster and Smith, (1987), has gone a good way in a tracking exercise that obviously needs regular updating. *Equality Assurance* (Runnymede, 1993) offers a comprehensive approach across the curriculum and an annotated sectional list of relevant resources.

The 1988 Education Reform Act

The developing focus on racism, sexism and on principles of equality and justice during the '80s influenced institutions across the country to adopt equal opportunities policies, at least on paper. Unfortunately, conservative governments have generally not been enthusiastic about principles of equality, and there may now be a trend towards eschewing such principles in favour of 'quality', 'efficiency' and 'value for money'. However, as argued in *Equality Assurance* and by Minhas in chapter 8 here, equality of opportunity must be addressed if quality in education is to be achieved.

Throughout the last decade we have seen legislation which has increased state influence in areas of civil life. The 'poll' tax and trade union reforms are examples. Education has been another arena for the government's political agenda, especially in reducing the power of its main opposition party in metropolitan areas.

Thus the 1988 Education Reform Act has reformed previous processes for the administration of education to make it more centrally prescribed, while appearing to offer more choice and power to the individual. The rationale upon which the reforms have been based are popular goals: of entitlement for every child to the National Curriculum, increasing parental choice and control in their children's education, and raising standards in education. Within the framework of the Act, the main processes by which these goals are to be reached are (a) local management of schools by their governing bodies (as against LEA management) and (b) the National Curriculum and Assessment.

We are nearly half a decade into the legislation taking effect and it is fair to say that full evaluation will necessarily take time. As far as children's entitlement is concerned, it is already clear that in practice there will not be similar access to the curriculum for all groups of children. Groups with disadvantages historically linked to poor socio-economic background, gender, ethnicity and language are not safeguarded from deficits in the system which have tended to compound their original disadvantage.

'Parental choice'

Overall parental choice and influence is likely to be diminished across all social groups. Practical experience points to the likelihood that families (if they are all not expected to get on their proverbial bikes), will still depend on places for their children at the nearest school. Shopping around for the best bargain is neither practically nor economically possible for most people. In reality it would appear that schools might now be choosing their pupils!

However, some parents will have the ability to choose better schools, and they will tend to be people in higher socio-economic classes. Two major effects can be anticipated from the exercise of this kind of advantage. One is that schools will become progressively divided along class lines. The second, evidenced in the Dewsbury and Cleveland cases, is that racism will have a new free ride in manipulating enrolment, and schools will tend to become divided along racial lines. Patsy Daniels, in Chapter 7, explains how the new arrangements for school governing bodies further threaten equal opportunities for black minorities.

'Raising standards'

The government's other main plank for the reforms is 'raising standards', partly by operating 'market forces' or competition through local management and the publications of Key Stage and public examination results achieved by each institution. Experience indicates that although schools may be enjoying increased autonomy over their finances and management, each institution has to put considerable resources towards complex administration systems, previously dealt with centrally by the LEA. This puts schools with less chances of financial backing, e.g. from better-off parents, at a disadvantage. Forced into competition with other schools for better academic results, selection at intake and banding will be strongly tempting, unless criteria for judging schools incorporates 'value-added' aspects. All these factors tend to adversely affect inner-city schools, and therefore those with large numbers of black children.

The role OFSTED, as Rehana Minhas explains in Chapter 8, will be paramount in drawing a high profile for the grounds on which schools are failing black children. Already there have been potentially influential reports from OFSTED incorporating these areas of weakness. The most recent, *Educational Support for Minority Ethnic Communities* (OFSTED, 1994) identifies successful practice by schools and LEAs in their use of Section 11 grant monies (See Chapter 9). The next few years will demonstrate OFSTED's actual impact on central policy and practice as well as that of schools.

Two other measures share a similar government rationale of 'raising standards'. One is reforming initial teacher education so that a major part takes place in the domain of schools rather than higher education institutions. The other is introducing regular appraisal of teachers, with an implication that salaries might become performance-related. There may be a case for increasing the practical classroom-based elements of teacher education, and for using appraisal positively for professional and institutional development. But where are the safeguards against unfairness and discrimination? The position of black teachers, for example, already documented as undermined through racism (CRE, 1988), could become much worse under the new measures.

At face value, the declared goals of raising standards and extending parental choice are shared by everyone. However, the means or processes by which the goals are said to be achievable are in doubt. If the processes, by their nature, invite the operation of biases (by ethnicity, gender; class, and so on), then we are in danger of producing results with undesirable differentials. Some schools, particularly in prosperous areas, will already have 'better' resources, support, teachers, reputations, and be better able to maintain their edge on other schools, the bottom strata of which, without intervention, will remain less able to give children a fair deal. In relation to ethnicity, the way seems even more open now for racial and cultural discrimination in many contexts.

The main concern of this book is the way the National Curriculum and its assessment impacts on black pupils. They affect *all* pupils similarly with regard to:

- whether the content of the curriculum is appropriate in scope and materials

- whether the range of teaching styles used for delivery motivates learning

- how and when, and the purposes for which, learning is assessed

In considering these issues in relation to black children, however, the challenge to the long-established child-centred approach is complex and demanding for teachers. Their awareness of each child's learning needs requires enough knowledge about individual linguistic and cultural backgrounds for them to be able sensitively to take these into account in planning for teaching, learning and assessment processes. There are several ways in which the National Curriculum and its assessment have tended to militate against the teacher taking account of these considerations.

Curriculum content has been inflexibly prescribed in its quantity and sequencing of Statements of Attainment (SoAs), now Level Descriptions. Teachers have been obliged, to be concerned with ticking off the numerous 'Statements' or 'descriptions' in endless boxed record sheets. How then could they concentrate on the more important and also time-consuming judgements about how best to motivate and progress each individual's learning? It is little wonder that after two years of desperately attempting to satisfy original expectations of the official authors of the National Curriculum, the volume of protests from teachers grew and culminated in the wide-spread boycotts of the Key Stage 3 tests in Summer, 1993 and to a large extent in 1994.

Dearing Review and Report

The government was obliged to acknowledge the need for a review of the National Curriculum and assessment and Sir Ron Dearing was appointed to head this task. For the first time the teaching profession was approached for their views. Dearing's preliminary findings were that the curriculum and assessment requirements were overloaded and would need slimming down to become more manageable.

The final Dearing Report proposed a reduction of the mandatory curriculum, especially outside the core subjects, leaving a theoretical average 20% of time for teachers to use at their own discretion. The number of Statements of Attainment for subjects would be reduced but the 10-level scale retained. The new curriculum was to be finalised by the end of 1994 and introduced in September 1995.

Although the review has gone some way towards appeasing angry teachers in reducing work-load, fundamental issues e.g. content in particular subjects, the fact is that the validity of the 10-level scale across all subjects and the appropriateness of some of the Attainment Targets and SoAs or Level Descriptions, have not been addressed. Teachers have found that not much has changed. Requirements are still relatively inflexible and administratively burdensome, particularly now that teacher assessment is to be more extensively part of Key Stage assessment .

Of most concern to us here, the Dearing Report took no account of bilingual children (except in Wales) and their language development (see chapters 3 and 5). In such a scenario teachers are unlikely to have the time or the inclination to incorporate content of relevance or interest to minority groups of pupils. They seem obliged to keep within the confines of a National Curriculum and assessment programme that in itself makes little attempt to accommodate cultural and linguistic diversity. These issues are taken up in more detail in later chapters.

Chapter 2

An inexact science
— issues of assessment

Pauline Lyseight-jones

The achievement or underachievement of our children presents us with complex, many-layered problems. As demonstrated throughout this chapter, social
science research can show association but cannot with certainty prove causality. Children from ethnic minority backgrounds are part of many other
subgroups too, determined by gender, by religious, class and economic background, by physical, intellectual or academic ability, by the styles of parenting
of their families. Consequently, some of the factors which impinge on the life
of a girl or the life of a wealthy child may also be part of the picture of a
particular child from an ethnic minority background.

Our children operate in many dimensions. The way that these dimensions
relate one with another is our puzzle and deep interest.

A brief glimpse at history
The children currently in the British system of education who come from ethnic
minority backgrounds are but the most recent of a range of migrations of
peoples to these islands. Polish and Czech people, Caribbean people, Kenyan
and Ugandan people, Pakistani and Bangladeshi people, Somalian and Eritrean

people are among the many who have settled in Britain. They leave the lands of their birth for a variety of reasons. Their arrival in Britain and the reception they receive will be coloured by the reasons for their movement and by cultural factors. Sympathy or tolerance may be the first outwardly expressed feelings to incomers but, regardless of the initial reception, immigrant groups will at some time feel isolated, rejected or ostracised and will eventually encounter disrespect from the larger community. These factors may make the immigrant group dysfunctional or ensure that it locks into itself to gain strength and support.

Even with the probability of a less than happy experience of becoming part of British society, immigrants in Britain usually have an advantage over the receiving community — they know more about Britain and the ways of its people, than the British know about *their* backgrounds. For example, the immigrant will know that English is the language of England, that England has a monarchy and that most people live in houses. Many teachers might not know the home language of the ethnic minority children they teach, whether their country of origin (or their parents' country of origin) is a republic, a monarchy or an autocracy nor what kind of shelter is usual for the majority of the population. This kind of lack of knowledge and curiosity about people may be the legacy of Empire. Unfortunately, such attitudes were exported when Britain sent its sons and daughters to settle in other lands. Terman wrote in 1916 that a low level of intelligence...

> is very common among Spanish-Indian and Mexican families of the South-west and also among Negroes. Their dullness seems to be racial or at least inherent in the family stocks from which they come... The writer predicts that... there will be discovered enormously significant racial differences in general intelligence, differences which cannot be wiped out by any scheme of mental culture.

> Children of this group should be segregated in special classes... they cannot master abstractions but they can often be made efficient workers... There is no possibility at present of convincing society that they should not be allowed to reproduce, although from a eugenic point of view they constitute a grave problem because of their unusually prolific breeding.

In 1927 sterilisation laws in parts of the USA established as legal fact the core assertion of biological determinism: that degenerate characteristics were transmitted through the genes. Such degenerate characteristics included 'criminals, epileptics, drug fiends and drunkards'. (In the event, the sterilisation programme targeted the whites in the Southern States, with the aim of 'purifying' the 'white race.')

The purpose of offering this brief background is to emphasise that irrational viewpoints may have behind them the forces of respectability that scientific enquiry endorses. Progress away from those views on to more accurate standpoints and conclusions does not mean that the original views have been entirely eradicated or forgotten. They live in the folk or cultural memory as a nagging doubt.

Today few would claim that IQ difference (that is, academic intelligence) between ethnic groups was genetically based. Clearly, the environment, the nurture aspect, is of great importance. Early development of testing systems ignored this factor.

Thus, during World War 1, the (US) Army Alpha test asked Polish, Italian and Jewish immigrants to identify the product manufactured by Smith and Wesson and to give the nicknames of players in a professional baseball team. For immigrants who could not speak English, the (US) Army Beta test was designed as a 'non-verbal' measure of 'innate intelligence'. That test asked the immigrants to point out what was missing from each of a set of drawings. The set included a drawing of a tennis court with the net missing. The immigrants who could not answer questions of this kind were thereby shown to be genetically inferior to the tennis-playing psychologist who devised such tests for adults.

This story of test development continues. It charts tests designed to ensure fairness to both boys and girls but still includes items which throw up differences of performance between social classes or between ethnic groups precisely because it is these differences in knowledge that the tests are meant to measure.

Tests are designed to discriminate between factors and groups. They may be designed as measuring tools. People came to test-design and test-development with their own prejudices. If test designers presume that different populations are similar or expect that different populations should operate to the conventions and mores of only one societal group then the designer will also expect that the results of the tests which they design should be treated as valid even when they cannot be so.

More recent research looks at a wide range of factors when considering cognitive attainment among children: social background and income are good predictors. Family variables, such as size and birth order, also appear to be related to educational outcomes. Again, while it is clear that there is an association or relation between these factors and attainment, actual causality or its mechanics are not proven.

The issue of race and achievement has been extensively debated (Rampton 1981, Swann 1985, Eggleston 1986, Tomlinson 1990). Within that discussion has been the ever-present spectre of under-achievement. This has the potential to present us with problems. What if children given special support by, say, Section 11 funding, achieve as well as their peers or better — do we applaud their teachers and take away the support, applaud the children and take away the support, or say 'there must be some mistake' and keep the support? Reports from the old Inner London Education Authority and from the present Inner London Boroughs on the achievement of children in public examinations seem to be showing a picture of achievement which does not put black children, as a homogeneous group, at the bottom of the heap. So what do we do now?

Perception

How we view our world and how we view the world of others makes a difference to our expectations of ourselves and of others. We, as teachers, still tend to have a notion of what our position is in society — and the parents of children whom we teach have similar personal, perceptual frameworks. I believe that there are two main prevailing perceptions which parents hold of their children and their children's achievements.

The first is that the child will achieve no more than the parent. This notion is founded on issues of self-esteem, 'what's wrong with our way of life' and on a wish for children to fit into society — to be happy and not to be hurt.

The second is that the child should achieve more than the parent, but not much more. This is not due to low expectations but to lack of knowledge of other opportunities. I shall try to explain what I mean. Firstly, consider three adolescents with similar achievements and academic ability: the student who went to a secondary modern school or was not in the top stream of the comprehensive might be advised to be a bank clerk, the student in the top stream or who attends grammar school might be advised to be a bank manger, while the student at public school might be expected to enter banking as a merchant banker in the City of London. Or take Pools winners. On winning a vast amount of money the pools winner's next move is almost always to a house that is one better than the one they live in at the moment. So, terraced becomes semi-detached with a bigger garden or more bedrooms. The knowledge of the breadth of possibilities is not there yet and, like many previously fat people who have slimmed but still go through doors sideways, they can't see themselves properly yet.

You may be thinking that some parents hold totally unrealistic expectations of their children — the cliché is that they want them to become brain surgeons.

It is possible that you are trapped in your own perception of relative values and that the parent is not. Or that the parent's background and contacts belie their present economic status. I have never met a brain surgeon — and don't know where you'd have to aim to enable someone to become one. The term 'brain surgeon' serves as an icon for the unattainable and the excellent, the precise and the difficult.

Given these two parental perceptions, if you as teacher had suggested that a child became, say, a cartographer or a chartered engineer and a parent rejected your suggestions as unrealistic — who would have been right?

A little story about expectations

Well, three stories. You may be wondering when the discussion about assessment issues begins — but, I assure you, assessment issues are precisely what we have been considering all along.

The pressures of society and its models mould us as children and adults. The issue, as usual, is power and the secret is the unwitting and unreflected activity as a result of our moulding — the effect that that activity has on our own aspirations and the aspirations of others:

A present-day problem

Story 1:

There is a school which has a swimming pool. All the children, throughout their four years at school (it's a middle school, 8-12) regularly have swimming lessons.

There are many children at the school whose family background is South Asian.

The headteacher and the deputy headteacher demonstrated by wiggling their ankles 'why Asian children can't learn to swim'. It seems it is because their ankles are too slim. The swimming coach had said so. The Asian children at that school either couldn't swim or couldn't swim well.

Therefore, the senior staff's expectations were confirmed by the evidence of their own experience.

Story 2:

One day, a while before John Major became Prime Minister, a ten-year-old boy was watching the television. A film of Margaret Thatcher was being shown. The boy asked his mother who she was. She said, 'The Prime Minister' and then, as parents do, asked him: 'Do you want to be Prime Minister when you grow up?' The boy answered, 'Don't be silly, men can't be Prime Minister'.

Story 3:

Research has shown that men and women show different patterns of response to job advertisements. An advertisement was put out, with the offer of good pay, and the vast majority of the applicants were men. When the identical advertisement appeared, with exactly the same wording, presentation and job description but the pay indicated as conservative to low, the majority of applicants were women.

Our society is presently grappling with the notion of relative poverty — poverty not as a static factor relating to a basic life-kit, but poverty that relates to the extent to which one's material circumstances allow one to be part of the generality of the society in which one lives. Poverty in Britain could be said to exist when one cannot afford to have a television, or take one's children out on occasional day trips, or have more than one pair of shoes and a selection of clothes for different circumstances and settings. Clearly, these are not the criteria that would currently pertain to Bosnian or Russia, nor to Kuwaiti nationals, in their home countries.

This relativity also operates in the perception of academic achievement by our children. There is a concept of relative achievement.

The time has long passed when the illiterate and the innumerate could expect to find jobs for which these learned skills were not necessary. Not only does the modern world require the graduates of its schools to be literate and numerate, it expects still more: technological and scientific capability, for example. In some areas of the curriculum, work which was once in the syllabus for undergraduates is now offered and expected to be understood by much younger school pupils. Children are required not just to be able to read and write but to write for a range of audiences and to analyse texts and their own use of language. Children (and adults) used to be able to get by on far less knowledge. Our children are not any less able than previous generations but we and our society are asking more of them with each passing Education Act and each final Order. To stand still, relatively, they have to keep moving. (There is, of course, another side to this argument — that of the village fool 200 years ago who was, in fact a computer whiz except that computers hadn't been invented yet. I feel that many of us are born either before or after our time and experience sensations of being in the wrong place, being dysfunctional because of it). It is necessary for us to recognise that our children exhibit a wide range of potential. The curriculum we have to teach and assess will, therefore, show us only part of the picture, tell us only part of the story.

Thoughts on literacy

A major part of the educational agenda today is the teaching of English — not 'Language' but 'English'. In the National Curriculum Assessment children who have been given assistance to gain access to the National Curriculum by speakers of their home language may not be given such assistance when English is being tested. This is logical. Amongst law-makers and writers of circulars and regulations a canon is developing which has as its first principle: 'There is such a thing as universal literacy. It is achievable by doing these things in this sequence.' If we believe that a narrow approach to teaching will improve the possibility of best achievement of all of our children, we are wrong.

Four more little stories — what do these tell you about reading?

Story 1:

A boy of under two years was watching the television. Up on the screen came the number '2'. The boy immediately said 'Two'. The mother thought, 'Crumbs, this boy can read'. She further thought 'He's making associations of symbols as having meanings. I must make him some flash cards of familiar objects to build up his sight vocabulary' (well, she was a teacher). He was reading fluently before he began school.

Story 2:

A girl who had been a member of the public library since she was eight months old — who was surrounded by books and reading and words, and went to a stimulating nursery school — was not interested in learning to read...not even out of envy. Three weeks before she was due to start school she said, 'I want to learn to read'. Her mother took this as meaning, 'and I want to know how to read straight-away' and went out and bought a three-stage proprietary reading package. The little girl was reading well by the time she started school.

Story 3:

A teacher had a class of nine and ten year olds for two and half terms. During that time they had very little formal (that is, planned for) teaching. They spent the time fighting amongst themselves, throwing things at the teacher and generally being nuisances. When the teacher left, another teacher was drafted in to calm the class down. That teacher also had responsibility for testing the reading attainment of all children in the school annually and recording these as Reading Ages. The children in this neglected class made, with very few exceptions, phenomenal jumps of two, three and more years in their Reading Ages. Moreover, they sustained this gain throughout their primary school career. It would seem that when the children had got bored with turmoil, they read. They read what they liked, when they liked and for as long as they wished, with support from whom-so-ever (other than the teacher) in the classroom.

Story 4:

On one occasion I used an SRA Reading Laboratory which focused on Comprehension Skills. I used it with a new class of nine and ten year olds. I used it with scepticism. The system worked.

At the moment, Reading Recovery programmes are being given a very good press. I would suggest that if I, as a child, had 30 minutes daily, exclusive, focused time with my teacher, it would be amazing if I did not show progress in the focused-upon area. (This indicates the need for support staff to be timetabled to particular children and meticulously to plan the support they offer each child.) Individual support is what many parents can give to their own children but teachers clearly cannot give to classes of 30 children or more. Some educational objectives are impossible to achieve or are unreasonable, given the reality of the staffing and resourcing of so many of our schools.

Some practical points

Learning styles, like teaching styles, vary considerably. To be able to respond to children we need to know about them — who they are and the ways they learn. To know them we need to observe them. After observing them we need to plan for them.

Observe one child each day or observe one activity each day or ensure that there is a structure for conferring and consulting.

Certain children from ethnic minority backgrounds might need English Language support for some part of their school careers. They might also need support which could be termed induction. That is, guidance on and knowledge about how the school system works — its culture, norms and mores. Add the effects of dislocation or transition and we may discover that such pupils need special support. School staff need to devise effective methods of identifying, monitoring and supporting children with special educational needs. The distinction would need to be made, at the very least, between children whose academic potential is at least average but where more knowledge of English and induction into the system are needed, and children whose special needs include the possibility that they have a specific learning difficulty.

Support staff need to have programmes which support individual children or groups of children. Such programmes should be complementary to the main teaching programmes in which the child or children take part. So programme planning should, as far as possible, be done in conjunction with relevant class or subject teachers. All teachers who teach a child as part of timetabled provision should be contributing to the record-keeping, evidence-gathering, observation, assessment and reporting process.

In the case of secondary schools, cross-departmental meetings or *aides-memoire* circulated to all staff should focus on the special or technical language of each subject — its jargon. This would enable language support staff to pre-empt some needs and be part of a drive to make all teachers aware of the necessity to support children who have specific needs. It would help teachers to ensure that children were not unduly disadvantaged when taking part in the formal aspects of National Curriculum Assessment. At present, translations of technical terms may be used at end of KS3 assessment (though not in English) but not the translated definitions of the words. So meaning has to be transmitted, discussed and understood before the assessment is carried out.

If pupils are to be brought up to the assessment and have long or short term special educational needs or specific learning difficulties, it will be necessary for the whole battery of possible support to be in place throughout the greater part of their taught timetable and not just during end-of-Key Stage assessment. SCAA allows for a range of support to be offered at end-of-key stage assessment. This includes extra time, use of readers and amanuensis, transcription, translation, use of braille and so on. Such support should not come as an unfamiliar surprise to children — popping up only at end-of-Key Stage assessment time. If these supports are needed to help children attain their maximum at testing or assessment time, they can clearly also help children to achieve of their best on a daily basis.

Disapplication

So far we have looked at issues which affect teachers' decisions about the children in their charge and at some practical issues which surround assessment and the needs of children from ethnic minority backgrounds. Progressively that commentary has moved into the area of the statutory assessment process.

The 1988 Education Reform Act described a National Curriculum and stipulated that there would be an assessment process by which pupils would be formally assessed at the ages of 7, 11, 14 and 16. At all but age 7 the results would be reported. 'Reported' meant being published as individual school scores by national government.

It became clear that the National Curriculum was not a curriculum for all but a curriculum for 'those who are like us'. The people who put together the Bill and described Attainment Targets in National Curriculum subjects did not have children with severe learning difficulties in mind, nor the autistic nor the refugee nor the transient child, nor the child for whom English was not the home language, nor the hospitalised child. The assessment system, too, ignored such children. Teachers of children with severe or moderate learning difficulties are counselled to introduce a 'small steps' curriculum, breaking down the Statements of Attainment into even smaller bits. (These are scheduled to disappear following the Dearing review.) Reference Notes which accompany the end of KS1 assessment were introduced in 1992 by the School Examinations and Assessment Council (SEAC) to assist teachers in making modifications to the assessment for children with a range of special educational needs. Even so, the ten-level National Curriculum is now under attack from right- and left-wingers alike. The assessment system is being brought to its knees by the secondary school lobby (though there is a bitter-sweet justice in that, since it is a secondary school model National Curriculum) and SEAC quietly removed 'diagnostic' as one of the purposes of assessment — leaving only 'evaluative, formative and summative'.

The system of assessment was being asked to do too many things. Its greatest value, to my mind, was in assisting the individual teacher and the individual child and in creating common ground for discussion — teacher-to-teacher. Its major public use has been as part of National Government propaganda and the bread and meat of right-wing newspapers trying earnestly to batter so-called 'looney left' teachers, schools and authorities.

Many head teachers have had to consider whether, even with public accountability, it is right to put children through the National Curriculum Assessment. Many head teachers are saying that the activity is not appropriate for the needs of particular children. By mid 1993, rebellion against the tests was widespread among professionals.

Most children with Special Educational Needs can be brought to at least the foothills of the National Curriculum but they may not be able to be formally assessed. As the children get older, the case for disapplying some of them from elements of the National Curriculum or delaying the end of a Key Stage programme or disapplying them from the assessment process becomes more compelling. The decision making must take account of individual pupil stress and possible low attainment outcomes which become part of the school level results showing a less high attainment rate for the school as a whole. The alternative is for the child to follow an appropriate, non-NC programme with the child's parents being made aware of their progress in the areas which were to be focused upon. The number of pupils disapplied from the National Curriculum Assessment might reflect poorly on some schools.

Some school staff find pupils recently arrived in England a source of difficulty when it comes to end of Key Stage assessment. For some staff the answer is to disapply all of the children who are in this position. (Indeed, in the first year of KS1 assessment requests were made in at least one authority for all children for whom English was a second language to be disapplied from the assessment, regardless of the children's competence and fluency in English or how long the children had been in England.) Other school staffs put all bilingual children into a younger age group, arguing on both social and educational grounds. If the child really is a recent arrival, disapplication from the SATS or tests may indeed be appropriate but this would not and should not mean that teacher assessment should not take place. If the child has been put into a younger age group there is no disapplication process to follow, as the children will not have reached the end-of-Key Stage programmes of study. When they do, they will be older than their classmates but eligible to do the end-of-Key Stage Assessment administered to their classmates.

If the school judges that a pupil is still not able to take part in the formal end-of-Key Stage assessment at this point, then a special direction should be sought as part of the process towards giving the child a statement of special educational need.

The important issue here is to make sure that the school staff have appropriate support structures and strategies for its pupil intake. The assessment, observation, monitoring, reviewing and reporting systems must work, otherwise we could see a repetition of the pattern identified by Bernard Coard (1971). That is, children from ethnic minority backgrounds will be disapplied from the National Curriculum and/or its related assessment for no reason other than their ethnic origins. And as a consequence their life chances will be effectively altered — almost inevitably for the worse.

Some outcomes of National Curriculum Assessment

Earlier in this chapter we noted that causality is difficult to prove in social science research. In the words of one advisory teacher: 'A school finds that all of its children achieve well in science in comparison to another school. Most of the children at the school wear trainers. Therefore, trainers make you good at science'. Of course they don't. We must be careful of saying that one factor causes another. What we *can* say is that one factor might be associated with another, then use our own powers of analysis to consider whether and why there should be such an association and whether or not it is valid.

Analysis of one borough's end-of-Key Stage 1 assessment results has shown that being eligible for free school meals, having a home language which is not English and having received Section 11 support in the year of the assessment all have a negative effect on group scores. This does not mean that not giving children Section 11 support will increase their scores. It means, rather, that children who fall into these groups, *as a group*, achieve less well than their peers. We also find that girls *as a group* show higher achievement than boys as a group across all assessed subjects, but most strikingly in English. Birthdate has an effect on National Curriculum assessment outcomes: the younger children in the cohort, as a group, achieve less well than older children.

In our own work, we found that class size of 31 or more had a positive effect on assessment outcomes while vertical grouping had a negative effect. Our best investigations lead us to a possible explanation. Our schools with classes of 31 or over made the decision to group children in this way because of lack of physical space — not lack of teaching staff — therefore, such children were often receiving more than one full-time teacher's working time in their class. Vertically-grouped classes tended to be created when numbers of children in the year group affected had changed to such an extent that the school could only provide either an additional part-time teacher or reduce a full-time teaching post. This tended to mean that the vertically grouped class had one teacher managing two year groups. This was the outcome of management and financial factors, not a decision determined according to best curricular or teaching practice.

Before leaving the subject it is worth reading the following, from *Primary Education* (1965):

> The Special Problems of Wales
>
> The underlying principles of life and education are the same for Wales and England. It is the good fortune of the Welsh children that they can, throughout their lives, participate in two national cultures, both of which form part of the European tradition, and which have been inextricably associated with one another for many centuries. One of the central aims of Welsh schools must be to extended to Welsh children the benefits of association with England and its language and literature and participation in its intellectual achievement and, at the same time, to maintain and nurture their respect for the best of their particular heritage.

What do we need to do?

Firstly, there is no shortage of good practitioners, of printed resources nor of appropriate strategies for supporting children from ethnic minority backgrounds who have particular educational needs, whether long or short term. This point requires no labouring here. What we do need to do is to remain sceptical about the validity of the broad National Curriculum assessment outcomes while at the same time speculating 'what if it's all true?' and act as if it might be.

Each child has a social history known to their teachers, which describes hierarchy of achievement or educational expectation. Some children are expected to achieve more than others because of factors which have little or nothing to do with their own potential. This is a recipe for self-fulfilling prophecy and can even override all other conditions influencing each child's likely educational progress.

Research confirms lower achievement in certain groups of children and might link other factors with this low achievement (such as the low educational attainment of many mothers from Bangladesh). But this is not the same as causality.

Assessment results allow us to look more closely at groups who under-achieve and to consider why this should be so, while remembering always that each individual within that group will not necessarily exhibit the expected/predicted or recorded behaviour of the group. So at Key Stage 1, for example, a young boy whose home language is not English, who is taught in a class of under 30 which is vertically grouped, is eligible for free school meals and who has received Section 11 support in the last academic year, might achieve level 4 across the board. An older girl whose home language is English, who is taught in a class of 31 or more pupils of the same age and who does not need free school meals might achieve no more than level 1 throughout.

This is a blunt tool but not an irrelevant one.

Think again: 'what if the children who had Section 11 support because their home language wasn't English were found, as a group, to be out-performing their year groups — what would we do then?'

Assessment of school children is an inexact science. We are hampered in our endeavours by both the misconceptions of history and the misrepresentation of politics. Our children are owed more than this.

Chapter 3

Educational Responses to Linguistic Diversity

Updesh Porter and Pat Keel

When Rudolf Nureyev died, media reports made much of the fact that he spoke not only English and his mother tongue Russian but also French, Spanish and Italian. Yet how many children in our schools get credit for speaking a range of languages besides English? A strait-jacket National Curriculum fails to do justice to the linguistic diversity existing in schools in Britain, especially when the languages that the children speak do not happen to be European languages (see also Chapter 7).

One of the marked features of modern Britain is the multi-ethnic composition of its population, yet the place of languages other than English in the lives of school children has been seriously underestimated by educators. Various national and local research studies indicate the linguistic diversity in our schools. Surveys have shown (Linguistic Minorities Project, 1983, 1985; also LEA based surveys, e.g. in Bradford, Coventry, Haringey, Peterborough and Waltham Forest) that particularly in inner-city areas there are sizeable numbers of pupils who speak at least one language other than English at home. In 1980/81 Haringey was found to have over 30% bilingual children, and a local survey of Ealing in 1989 showed a percentage of 41.5.

At an official level it is acknowledged that we are a linguistically diverse nation but there is frequent evidence of ambivalences. For example, Swann states that:

> In order to lay the foundation for a genuinely pluralistic society the education system must, we believe, both cater for the linguistic needs of ethnic minority pupils and also take full advantage of the opportunities offered for the education of all pupils by the linguistic diversity in our society (Swann, 1985, chapter 7).

Similar sentiments supporting linguistic and cultural diversity are echoed in National Curriculum statements and guidance documents (see for example NCC Circular No. 11 and English Non-Statutory Guidance). However, official statements always stop short of adopting a really multilingual approach to language development. If we consider the battle over the English curriculum, it is clear that there are political forces that powerfully resist any broad approach to language.

English Curriculum

Before the advent of the National Curriculum, the government had set up a working party to make recommendations for the improvement of English language teaching — first under Kingman and later, Cox (LINC Project). The reports of both Kingman (see Bell, 1991, *Multicultural Teaching* 10.1) and Cox were disregarded and their approaches to language development, which would build pupils' awareness of the nuts and bolts of linguistic communication, were never put into practice on a national scale.

Some fifteen years earlier, Bullock (1975) suggested approaches to language by which every teacher would contribute to raising language awareness through their subject, and pupils would have their language developed across the curriculum. Hark at echoes in the National Curriculum:

> Language is the means of learning throughout the school curriculum and throughout every Key Stage. The Statutory Orders and the non-statutory guidance for Science, Mathematics and Technology emphasise this point. It is essential that opportunities are created to develop children's learning through language and as users of language, in all curriculum areas (para 1.1 English Non-Statutory Guidance A1).

and:

Pupils' knowledge about language is increased by discussion and analysis of their own use of language. They should develop an understanding of both the structure of language and how it is used (para 1.6 English Non-Statutory Guidance A1).

But if teachers have not been initially or subsequently trained to carry this out, aren't these just fine words? The LINC Project would have pupils developing an appreciation of the different registers and varieties of English in this country and beyond, so giving due recognition to regional accents and forms of expression. Such an approach has proved out of tune with the narrower emphasis required by the government on 'Standard English', which stresses 'correct' pronunciation, grammar and spelling (Cox, Dec. 1992, *Opinions*, Channel 4). The prescribed English Literature reading lists for Key Stage 3 are similarly restricted to an 'establishment' or traditional model, to which many people, including English teachers have responded with dismay.

The Dearing review elicited many well-argued representations which pleaded the necessity to consider the language development patterns of bilingual children (see also Chapter 5). The Draft Proposals for English have ignored these pleas. They reveal the same narrow perspectives as before, prompting a fresh round of protest.

Bilingualism

With such a narrow path being marked out for Language, it is not surprising that bilingual children are largely seen as a problem, even when they are being apparently positively considered The fact that in Wales bilingual education flourishes is presented as a situation peculiar to that part of the world! Only there are children's bilingual skills regarded as legitimate. Schools teach Welsh, English and other European languages and the curriculum is taught bilingually. The Welsh Language Education Development Committee, set up by the Government as a result of pressure in Wales, asserts that Welsh-medium instruction should be offered to every child, irrespective of age or ability. According to the *Times* (26.10.92):

> In the traditional rural Welsh-speaking heartland of Gwynedd and Dyfed, the education authorities aim to make every child bilingual by the age of eleven.

However, the lessons of the Welsh model have not been applied in England, where the intention has remained since the 1960s to assimilate bilingual children into a British curriculum, primarily by making them fluent in English.

All detailed advice (eg in Non-Statutory Guidance in the Programmes of Study, and in the NCC Circular No. 11 *Linguistic Diversity and the National Curriculum* and the School Assessment Folder — Key Stage 1) faintly disguise this intention. For example:

> Children come to school already with a background of language, sometimes more than one language. The programmes of study emphasise the need to build upon this and to provide children with opportunities to extend and develop their use of English (eg POS2 in AT1; POS2 in AT2; POS4 in AT3) (para 1.4 English Non-Statutory Guidance A1).

This does seem supportive of the children's first language, but if there is a complete absence of first language teaching, particularly at primary level, then how can a teacher be sure that the first language is fact being developed and is capable of being built upon? Isn't the main stress on the requirement to 'extend and develop their use of English'? The same appears to be true of the following:

> In Key Stage 1, particularly, the knowledge parents have of their child's development is indispensable to teachers. Where children are new to English, their families will be an important source of information about their competence in their first language (para 1.5 English Non-Statutory Guidance A1).

If this is a recognition of the wealth of language with which some children arrive, and that skills in home languages should be used as the foundation for English language development, then a model of this approach was provided by the Primary Language Record introduced by ILEA, which was welcomed by many teachers as incorporating a sensitive framework for promoting the language development of children new to English. Valuing and supporting bilingual development was central to ILEA's approach. Teachers were encouraged to consult parents regularly about their child's progress in school and at home.

Of course families should be drawn into involvement with their children's education in the way suggested by the Guidance, but this advice needs to be matched with actual support for 'their competence in their first language'. Also the area of home-school links is one which lacks central thought, advice and staffing. Again, an INSET programme should be instigated to support all teachers in putting such links into action. The processes by which home-school links are successfully built with ethnic minority parents and communities are not appreciated fully in many schools. The Intercultural Education Project which grew out of the Collaborative Learning Project has a strong focus on home-school liaison.

Even when teachers have the utmost sympathy towards valuing and supporting bilingual development it is difficult to sustain this in the classroom when there is no central policy nor the backing of resources. That policy must be concerned, as Robinson (1985) points out, 'with the linguistic needs of bilingual children both in terms of the acquisition and use of English and also in terms of the acquisition, use and maintenance of their mother-tongues.'

Robinson observes that 'the fact that most of the children from ethnic minorities are bilingual or bidialectal has largely been ignored'. The school's response, often through multicultural policies promoted in the 1980s, addressed issues only at a 'rather superficial' level. He argues that 'the real issue of multicultural education, that of linguistic diversity, has been almost totally neglected'. For education the significance of multilingual communities poses too many problems. The issue is further contaminated by confrontational politics: the hard right has located issues of equality and justice in the left-wing camp and lumped in 'ethnic minority' issues.

Language Status

Besides, deeply held prejudices carry over into negative attitudes to the language of black people. Terms such as 'mumbo-jumbo' and 'double dutch' are not used by coincidence. European languages are named Modern Foreign Languages in the secondary curriculum and the languages of ethnic minorities are called Community Languages. Although there is now parity in examination status, there are disincentives for secondary schools to offer examinations. It is legally required that the school should have the staff and resources to offer a Modern Language first of all, before the school can make arrangements to cater for pupils' choices of Community Language.

Unfortunately these attitudes regarding English as the dominant language and the general knowledge base have affected the pupils in school. Within one generation in a community like Southall, a language 'shift' has taken place. Children prefer to speak English at home rather than Panjabi. Educationists are aware of these 'transitional' bilingual communities and research (Tosi, 1982) has shown that children in these communities go through a period of 'semi-lingualism'. They are neither fully proficient in their mother tongue nor in English and their cognitive development is consequently vulnerable.

The DES-funded Mother Tongue and English Teaching Project in Bradford (MOTET, 1979-80) examined the value of using the first language as well as

English in the early years of schooling. The experimental group was taught through the medium of Panjabi for half the day and in English for the rest.

> Not only did the experimental group develop their mother tongues to a far greater degree than had the control groups, their acquisition of English had not suffered; on the contrary, their skills in English had developed slightly faster than those of the control groups (Rees and Fitzpatrick, 1981).

Studies in Canada, the United States, Europe and in this country have linked first language maintenance to positive effects on learning second languages and on achievement in general (eg the Bradford MOTET Project). Others suggest that bilingual skill may lead to higher levels of cognitive development (Vygotsky, 1962; Gregory and Kelly, 1994).

Resourcing First Language Maintenance

A frequent excuse for not providing bilingual education is the shortage of bilingual teachers, especially in schools where pupils speak a variety of languages. However, where there are major language groups in one region — eg Urdu in Bradford, Gujarati in Leicester and Brent, Panjabi in Ealing, Houslow and Birmingham, Bengali in London's East End, Turkish and Greek in North London — it is possible for local authorities to make provision for the maintenance of these languages.

Hargreaves (1983) found that: 'a large number of schools, understandably but disappointingly, feel that the problems involved in mother tongue provision are too complex to be coped with and do nothing'. ILEA's rich linguistic diversity in the classrooms was promoted effectively because of ILEA's intensively promoted equal opportunities policy. As Hargreaves explains:

> We remain very firmly convinced that mother tongue provision is an essential ingredient in any programme designed to combat under-achievement amongst ethnic minorities and urge both divisional inspectors and divisional education officers to review current practice in their area with a view to improving access to provision.

Parents' views

Parents who are aware of these issues feel strongly about the maintenance of their language, culture and identity. The relationship between language and cultural identity is very important and they fear that their children are losing their identity and that their cultural values are declining. Rees (1984) believes that cultural identity and cultural values are expressed through a particular language:

> Experience in many bilingual societies suggests that ethnic identity and religious affiliation are bound up with language use and will tend to ensure the survival for long periods of time of the bilingual language of ethnic minorities.

From my experience of Panjabi in a high school in Southall, it was clear that parents and students saw the teaching of Community Languages as a means of achieving social and cultural harmony in their homes. A sixth former stressed the role of the home languages like this:

> When you are with you family and relations you speak your mother tongue. You don't speak English or French. Panjabi reminds you who you are because although you are living in England you are Asian, you are Panjabi, and your parents come from Panjab originally. It helps you to remember who you are. I would like to tell my children that they are not English as such. If you forget your language you lose a very big part of your culture.

Yet teachers often assume that, because some ethnic minority parents have no wish to see their home languages taught in the school and want their children to use only English, this is the view of all parents. The research of Verity Khan (1980) and Rees and Fitzpatrick (1981) suggest that it is not. Both parents and teachers need to develop their understanding of the issues involved in the use of more than one language in the school.

Deculturation and Assimilation

Hamers and Blanc (1989) argue that:

> In a harmonious acculturation process a person acquires cultural rules and integrates them appropriately with his primary culture. This leads to the development of a bicultural identity. But when an individual adapts to a new culture at the expense of his primary culture we speak of 'a process of deculturation.'

Deculturation would, then, eventually lead to assimilation. In any case the theory breaks down when skin colour and racism are also factors. School policies should be sensitive to the emotional dilemmas of children in their schools and should encourage harmonious amalgamation of two or more cultures into one's identity.

Cummins (1981) found that a common feature of ethnic minority students with academic problems is 'characterised in ambivalence towards the majority group and insecurity about the value of their own cultures' and even by being ashamed of their home language. And negative attitudes of teachers towards pupils who speak languages or even versions of English that differ from their own, means that children soon learn that their home language is not valued at school. Edwards (1978) argues that:

> Negative attitudes to language rather than linguistic deprivation may be responsible in part for the under-performance of West Indian children in British schools and there are strong links between attitudes towards language and attitudes towards speakers of that language.

Cox (1991) made clear in his report that it was impossible to prescribe a single policy for the teaching of English for all schools. His working group was sensitive to different views of the main aims of English teaching. One of the aims, he said, 'is to add Standard English to the repertoire, not to replace other dialects or languages'.

According to Edwards (1978) the poor educational performance of African-Caribbean students is associated with their low esteem and feelings of inferiority towards their own dialects. The pattern of 'bicultural ambivalence' can also be seen among black, Mexican-American students in the USA and is traced to the historical tradition of segregation and discrimination. On the other hand, Skutnabb-Kagas and Toukomma (1976) showed that Mexican-American and Finnish immigrant students who immigrated after several years of schooling in their home countries, achieved higher academic performance than those born within a minority context. Could this be the reason that Vietnamese children appear to achieve so well in education in England?

Morrison (TES 14.6.91) found out through An Viet, a cultural organisation which compiles statistical information about Vietnamese educational achievements, that 70% of the 500 who passed A-levels in 1990 went on to high education. Of those, 20% went to Oxbridge, 20% to London and just under half to redbrick universities. Of the 1984 intake into university, when most had been in this country for only a few years, eleven Vietnamese have now completed doctorates and 40 are about to do so.

Underachievement

At a national level the main issue with which virtually all the media have been occupied regarding the education of ethnic minorities has been their under achievement. The smaller body of research into the achievement — or other-wise — of the *providers* of education: Coard (1971), Stone (1981), Eggleston (1986), Smith and Tomlinson (1989), Gillborn (1990) has received far less attention. This may have something to do with the fact that all these researchers eschewed the model of the 'underachieving pupil' and focused instead on the attitudes, policies and practices of the teachers and schools, demonstrating their discriminatory outcomes. The Swann Report (1985) was again concerned with underachievement and, as we have seen, while making positive references to minority languages, considered 'language' largely in the context of English. For instance:

> The English language is the central unifying factor in 'being British', and is the key to participation on equal terms as a full member of this society (Swann, 1985, chapter 7).

It has been rightly pointed out that the Report 'ignores the pluralist values underlying the multilingual approach to language policies and mother-tongue teaching in particular' (Khan, 1985). In 1990 the Home Office revised its Section 11 funding arrangements in education (see Chapter 9 for fuller discussion of Section 11) and once again concern for the underachievement of ethnic minorities is expressed:

> The Government's aim is to help the members of such communities to benefit fully from opportunities for educational, economic and social development. To this end the grant has provided and will provide support in the teaching of English, in strategies aimed at improving educational performance... (Home Office, 1990)

These guidelines leave no room for the possibility of bilingual approaches either to language learning or to education in general. The Home Office Guidelines state that money will not be given to local authorities for pro-grammes aimed at raising achievement through multicultural approaches:

> The Government fully recognises the benefits that derive from the main-tenance of religious, artistic, cultural and linguistic traditions among ethnic minority communities. It does not, however, consider Section 11 grant to be an appropriate use for initiatives aimed a such purposes.

The Home Office expects linguistic and cultural maintenance to be the responsibility of the communities themselves.

Assessment of Bilingual Pupils

In Chapter 5 Maggie Gravelle and Elaine Sturman explain how the School Assessment Folder Key Stage 1 fails to make adequate provision for their statutory assessment and how bilingual skills and linguistic understanding are discounted. As Stubbs (1989) observes:

> Bilingual children do not anywhere (in the National Curriculum requirements) get credit for their knowledge of two or more languages... The assumption appears to be that bilingual education in Britain is ruled out and that English should become the 'first language' of the children themselves. Language loss appears to be recommended.

Moreover, teachers receive no national guidelines or training in the relevant area. They need to understand the processes bilingual learners go through in the development of their first and subsequent languages, since this has obvious implications for how they assess pupils, particularly in any summative assessment which is to be reported, e.g. the Standard Assessment Task results. So far class teachers rely totally on Section 11 teachers for this. Where there are only a few bilingual pupils in a school, they may be given no specialist support whatever. Secondly, the generally age-related SoAs and Standard Assessment Task results do not allow for particular stages and processes of bilingual pupils' learning. As anyone with experience of learning a second language knows, it takes time to reach levels of competence. Research indicates that fluency in a new language takes between two to four years for most children.

The danger is that children who have had only two years of learning English and are struggling to master basic skills in English might be labelled as underachievers or as having special educational needs. The *Times Educational Supplement* (23.4.1993) noted:

> Some ethnic minority children are being wrongly assessed for special educational needs, because translators or interpreters are not available when statements are drawn up.

Equal opportunities and language policies

Throughout this book the issue of equal opportunities for multilingual pupils is a central theme. How can there be equality of entitlement to educational provision if children's home languages are in effect discounted? Speaking and learning one's own language is after all a matter of equal opportunities. Morrison and Ridley (1989) point out that 'the curriculum is value based. It is founded on the principle of protection and neglect of selected values'.

Language planning in England has been characterised by top-down directives from a government whose ideology includes 'linguistic assimilation' (Warhaugh, 1986). And as Shipman (1990) says 'majority teachers tend to follow a set of beliefs or values issuing from the dominant powers in society which has imperceptibly permeated the whole class structure'. Headteachers are now more concerned about the successful implementation of the National Curriculum, and the language needs of bilingual children are becoming invisible. Even Southall schools where Panjabi has been taught since the early '80s are tending to decide that they can no longer offer this subject.

However, despite the opposing official tide, many teachers in a fair number of schools across the country still work in excellent ways to encourage multilingualism. The National Association for Language Development in the Curriculum (NALDIC) is a group of such people, many of them teachers of English as a Second Language. There is a growing awareness of the extent and importance of pupil multilingualism. Strapped for cash as they may be, some LEAs still struggle to support bilingual pupils in precisely the ways set out in the 1993 School Assessment Folder — Key Stage 1 [para B.8] (See also Chapter 5). The list of strategies suggested as 'effective practice in the assessment of non-fluent children' is useful, if sometimes vague. It probably represents SEAC's hurried notes from consultation meetings held with teachers. However, there are serious resource and training implications for carrying out these strategies. The burden of responsibility for thier provision is blithely dumped on LEAs and schools.

Every government is concerned with creating its own vision of society. An attempt was made in the last decade to ignore teaching professionals and to take control of the curriculum. It is widely recognised that right wing pressure groups, notably the Centre for Policy Studies and the (overlapping) Hillgate Group have had a dominant influence on education policy (Bolton, 1992). Members of the CPS held key positions in NCC and SEAC and are now heavily represented in SCAA. The National Curriculum accordingly has a Eurocentric perspective, and English holds supremacy over the multitude of languages that exist in Britain today. Educational planners define policies within the marked out confines of their political masters.

Nonetheless, as they develop their IDPs and determine the content, aims and pedagogy of curricula, planners cannot afford to ignore the perspective of their multilingual pupils and their parents. As Robinson (op cit) suggests: 'it may not be possible to provide teaching in all these languages , but it certainly is possible to provide it for the major language groups'.

What kind of society do we want in the next century? If the economy of Britain is going to expand beyond Europe, will it not use the full resources of its citizens? Michael Marland (1985) reminded educationalists about the lack of vision in the approach of the USA to language and what happened as a result:

> It found to its horror that it has no speakers of a whole range of world languages. It had to start a crash course to make good the deficiency. If we get our languages teaching right we can have a generation coming out of schools who are bilingual and who will be a great asset to a commercial nation like ours.

It is important that in our vision of the future, we create an ethos in education that actively encourages everyone to increase their language awareness and make competence in more than one language a desirable goal. Leeds for example, has declared itself a 'multilingual city' and takes initiatives which promote this aspect of its life. In such an ethos we would all respect and value the use of minority languages and exploit the rich linguistic diversity of British classrooms. Bullock, nearly two decades ago, observed sadly that the value of bilingualism: 'is often ignored or unrecognised by the schools', and argued that 'in a linguistically conscious nation in the modern world we should see it as an asset, as something to be nurtured, and one of the agencies which should nurture it is the school'.

Chapter 4

Assessing young children's learning

Celia Burgess-Macey

The National Curriculum has focused public attention on assessment. There is also an increased interest in assessment among early years professionals. The Children Act has raised awareness of the need for greater partnership between agencies involved with young children and the value of developing compatible forms of record-keeping across different early years settings. A further incentive to focus more sharply on methods of assessment will come from the implementation in September of the Draft Code of practice for children with special needs. This will require detailed observations of children to be recorded at several different stages, both before and after the issuing of a statement of special educational need.

Early years practitioners have always kept records, often developed by themselves or with colleagues in the same LEA, mainly in order to help them understand and plan for children's progress. They have also kept records to share with parents and to pass on to the primary school or the next teacher, with the aim of ensuring continuity of learning for the child.

The current interest in baseline assessment in schools, however, arises from a different source. Schools feel the need to prove that they are teaching children effectively and that the learning that a child can demonstrate by the age of the Key Stage 1 tests and assessment has in fact been facilitated by the school. Without baseline assessment on entry to school the value-added component of a child's later performance cannot be calculated. Accordingly, many schools are introducing baseline assessment, or are requiring of pre-school settings that some form of record of achievement is transferred with the child.

Early years educators need to treat the issue of assessment very carefully. We need to be clear about which purposes of assessment we are working towards, and which models of the early years curriculum and of children's learning underpin our models of assessment. We cannot uncritically adopt a model handed down from National Curriculum and assessment procedures.

Positive underpinning

We may want to start by unpacking some assumptions.

> Our starting point is that children of all backgrounds and abilities bring with them, whenever they start school, a rich and individual collection of knowledge, skill, attitudes and experiences, and that if we are to devise a learning programme for the child starting school which builds directly on 'where the child is' we need to have some kind of systematic and professionally valid way of documenting that competence and experience...We need to be sensitive to the full range of knowledge children might bring with them. We need to know where and when to look...we need to know how to describe it...we need the skills to uncover the culturally embedded knowledge and meanings which young children possess, and to do so in rich detail and without judgement (Stierer et al, 1993).

If we are assuming, as Marian Whitehead (1994) does, that young children are experts in three main areas of understanding — the linguistic, the interpersonal and the representational — then the curriculum we construct will, as she says, be 'radically different' from the National Curriculum. (For detailed descriptions of the early years curriculum see Blenkin and Kelly, 1988 and EYCG, 1989 and 1992.) It follows that the way we assess and what we record will also be radically different. Whitehead argues that:

> The daily and often undervalued mix of play, language and social skills is the real foundation of cognitive development: — its components are more truly described as the basics than the usually cited conventions of written language and mathematical notation.

To assess children's development properly we must, she believes, adopt a holistic approach both to individual children and to knowledge ...an approach which recognises that 'children are already on their way to becoming thinkers, readers and writers in their homes and communities' (Whitehead, 1994).

PROCESS Records

It is this holistic approach to children as learners that has underpinned the development of approaches to assessment developed by Stierer *et al* at Roehampton Institute and the London Borough of Merton in the PROCESS record (Profiling, Recording, Observing Competencies and Experiences at the Start of School). Instead of focusing attention on a checklist of specific skills, this record encourages adults to comment on learning under the following headings: interaction, attitudes, investigating and problem solving, communicating, representing and interpreting; and also to comment on individual approaches and needs, special interests or knowledge, languages spoken and understood and physical development.

The summative record is closely related to ongoing observations of children, and three significant observations are to be selected from the ongoing records and transferred to the summative record. The handbook explains the ways in which the headings used overlap with several subject areas of the National Curriculum and help to place children's progress and achievements in Attainment Targets in a proper context of assessment of the whole child.

Primary Learning Records

Another very positive approach to assessing young children is that taken by the Centre for Language in Primary Education and pioneered in their much copied Primary Language and Primary Learning Records. The approach is well summarised in the handbook:

> Records need to keep a balance between the child centred and subject centred approaches to learning and to provide qualitative descriptions of learning to go alongside detailed accounts of curricular achievement. Record keeping helps teachers to consider how children are learning so that they will be in a better position to support that learning. In *Patterns of Learning* the model of learning is described as a continuum made up of five dimensions. These dimensions provide an explanatory framework for understanding and analysing children's development and progress (Hester, 1993).

Staff using the Primary Learning Record are encouraged to observe the process of children's development in confidence and independence, experience, strategies used, knowledge and understanding and reflectiveness.

Several LEAs have adopted a similar approach in their early years records. They stress the importance of careful observations of children in a variety of normal learning contexts. Records highlight processes of learning and thinking which are cross-curricular and recursive, and include the perceptions of parents (Kensington and Chelsea, Sheffield, Greenwich). The approach adopted could be described as a profiling approach in that the record is built up over time through observational evidence.

At a more polemical level, Myra Barrs, in *Words not Numbers* (1990), argues cogently against models of assessment based on measuring performance against smaller and narrower set pieces of knowledge and discreet easily measurable skills and ignoring the broader picture, the underpinning processes of thinking and attitudes to learning. She argues for an approach founded on our own developing understanding of children as learners. This understanding cannot be summed up by any checklist but can only be built up over time through observation of children in a variety of contexts using a variety of strategies.

Parental partnership

The Primary Language Record recognises the importance of early years professionals taking parents and carers into partnership and acknowledging that their knowledge of their child should be the starting point of our record. Partnership is more honoured in the breech that the observance and this initial parent conference might perhaps be the last until the child is about to leave the class. This is an appalling waste of parents' insights. It is also a waste of our insights, which if they were regularly shared with parents, could stimulate parents to look at their child's learning in new and exciting ways.

There are very important equalities issues in working with parents. Children's learning is contextualised within their cultures at home as well as within the cultures of school. As professional educators we need to be aware of the learning that children demonstrate in those very different contexts and of the different content of that learning. Children do not perform at their best in unfamiliar environments and may be unwilling to share what they know and can do in situations where the adults are unaware of or unsympathetic to their cultures.

Chris Athey describes how this became apparent in her child studies and in working with parents:

In the project, aspects of early learning were illuminated by studying children from very different socio-economic backgrounds. It gradually became apparent that schematic behaviours were common to both groups as was some everyday content. Some content, however, reflected different experiences...In a culturally diverse society, different interpretations of apparently common events amount to different experiences. The dear little pink pig of European children's literature's (and included in intelligence tests) will be viewed somewhat differently by Muslims (Athey, 1990).

The partnership approach has been adopted very successfully in Pen Green (a nursery and family centre in Northamptonshire). Staff there use the schema approach developed by Chris Athey and explained in her book, *Extending thought in young children*. More recently Cathy Nutbrown has expanded this approach in *Threads of Thinking (1994)*. Parents are encouraged to observe and record any preoccupations with schema (enclosing, rotation, grids etc) in the behaviour of their children. Likewise the observations of staff about children's developing schema is fed back to parents in a continuous dialogue. Even children themselves are involved and can impress visitors by fetching their own profile file and talking with pride and confidence about the record of their achievements. This has meant that staff have shared with parents a view of an early years curriculum and a view of children's development.

The development of the PACT reading record is an example of another pioneering attempt to take parents into partnership as regards the development of their children as readers, and in many London boroughs the PACT parent handbooks have been translated into community languages to facilitate communication. Research has shown the benefits to the children's performance as readers. What is less obviously counted, but equally significant, are the benefits that can be gained because the parent is allowed an insight into the processes of professional assessment as they apply to her own child.

The Primary Language Record also pioneered the recognition of children's cultural and linguistic knowledge as being a proper concern of teachers. Until then the tendency was for teachers to expect that the children left their language and culture at the classroom door, hung up with their coats. It should have been obvious that this was not only ignoring an invaluable asset, it was also a discriminatory practice. It denied some children equal access to a curriculum and to motivating learning experiences that built on their own previous learning and which keyed into their interests and concerns. If a child is assessed in the context of a curriculum that has little relevance and which has not connected with her own prior learning, that child will not perform to the best of her potential.

KPAG

I have taken two examples of baseline assessment records to look at more critically. The first is the Keele pre-school assessment guide, KPAG, which was designed for use in nursery classes to plot the progress of individual children. In the explanatory notes it is also suggested that the record can be used 'to provide an outline of and suggestions for activities in pre-school setting.' Although users are warned against the 'teaching to the test' approach, the arrangement of a record of this kind does in practice lend itself to that approach.

Staff are required to award levels of competence on a five point scale. Items are placed in categories of cognitive, social, physical and linguistic skills. The selection of items to be included was based on existing psychological tests and assessment charts and on research in child psychology, eg Piaget, Cazden. In other words the assessment advocated is based on a psychological not an educational model. The dangers of psychometric testing have been well researched and cannot be discussed here (see Bourdieu, Goldstein (1991); Broadfoot, Labov (1969); Gipps (1990) etc). What this leads to is the selection of items according to their validity as test items, not according to their validity to children.

A Reductionist Approach

So we have lists of items taken out of context. There is a real danger at present that many early years professionals will have a reductionist approach to assessment imposed on them — simple checklists of skills which measure what is easy to measure but which neglect to record the more complex processes of a young child's developing understandings which in fact are far more interesting and informative.

For example in the section on cognition under the category 'Space and Time', the following prompts appear:

> Name the days of the week. To score this the child must be able to name three days of the week when asked to do so. If the child does not respond say 'You know the days have names like Monday...can you tell me other names?' The item is to be credited if the child gives three further names.

and

Differentiate between left and right
This item is to be scored if the child responds correctly to *all* of the following commands/questions
    Show me your right hand
    Which is your left ear?
    Raise your left arm
    Point to your right foot.

Knows today, tomorrow and yesterday:
credit this item if the child is able to name correctly today and name yesterday or tomorrow.

The inadequacy of simplistic assessment models when dealing with young children's approaches to reality are encapsulated in the poem quoted by Marian Whitehead (1994):

He knew a lot of time: he knew
Gettinguptime, timeyouwereofftime,
Timetogohometime, TV time,

Time for my kisstime (that was Grantime),
All the important times he knew,
But not half-past two.'

U.A. Fanthorpe, 1992

Any assessment process that places the child in a test type situation of responding to questions and tasks that have been devised by the adult and *have no inherent meaning for the child* must be resisted. We are asked to assess learning that is de-contextualised from any concrete and meaningful situation. Margaret Donaldson (1978) has shown that this is very misleading. Piaget's famous test, purporting to show that young children cannot decentre, required a child to look at a model of a hill and try to describe the position of the house on the other side. If the test is repeated in the context of a storytelling that makes sense to a young child, the child does not become confused and can decentre very well. At a cultural level this also applies. A child will perform better in those activities that have meaning in their own culture (Brice Heath, 1983).

Cultural Bias
Let me take another example from Keele, this time from the section on language development. The list of items includes: *'Knows own name and several nursery rhymes'*.

Which children will be likely to perform well on this? Naturally, the children who know English nursery rhymes will tend to come from white, English middle class homes. If we were to ask: *Knows names and words of several popular songs or hymns,* we would get different responses. What then does this test really tell us about language? The next question at the next level of difficulty asks the child to: *'repeat six nursery rhymes fairly accurately.'*
What if the child comes from a culture where nursery rhymes are not valued but the Koran or Christian hymns might be?

The next question is: *'Able to hold a coherent and lengthy conversation.'* The instructions read:

> This item is very strictly scored. Credit is only to be given if child frequently holds conversations with adults and other children lasting several minutes on diverse subjects and with coherent expressions of thought.

Children from backgrounds where adult/child exchanges are of a different nature than those described here will not achieve or perform well in tests of this kind. But this does not mean that their language is deficient. It does mean that the contexts in which their linguistic competence will be best displayed will be different, as Labov (1969) found with the black New York children judged by teachers to be deficient in their language development but who were totally competent verbally in the playground.

Socialisation

The section on socialisation is equally instructive. Who decided that the most significant indicators of early social interaction include: 'Washes hands satis-factorily and uses knife, fork and spoon' (but presumably not chopsticks), or that looking at children playing together so as to assess whether they *'under-stand the concept of winning and losing'*. Is this really significant? I can think of many adults who would fail on that!

Should we really be happy to score a child an a scale of 1-7 as : *'aggressive, often involved in quarrels'* to *'timid, avoids conflict'*? Is this judgement to be made irrespective of the situation? Are we to assume that a tick at either end of the scale is a bad thing? Black children in particular have been labelled on these 'social behaviour measures' and time and again teachers have failed to take into account the context of racism within which they operate. The racism of their peers may well render positive assertion (often interpreted as aggres-sion), or even outright aggression an appropriate, or at least understandable response. And there are other children for whom timidity will be an appropriate response to a strange and demanding environment not in sympathy with their cultural background. Unfortunately, far from being discredited, the reductionist and selective approach legitimated in KPAG is receiving a new impetus in approaches to baseline assessment which are strongly influenced by the Attainment Targets of the National Curriculum.

Wandsworth Baseline Checklist.
The Wandsworth Baseline Checklist has been developed as an entry assessment for children in their first term of school. It includes a section on 'Background biography', with one line spaces for main language spoken at home, special needs or aptitudes ('musically gifted' is the only example quoted) and a one line space for summary of pre-school provision. There is space to record social and emotional development, independence and ability to concentrate, perseverance and relationships with pupils and adults are listed under this heading. It is not clear why these are categorised as social and emotional and not as educational/conceptual.

It is when we get to the headings that have most similarity to subjects of the National Curriculum that the record's purpose becomes apparent. The headings chosen correspond to the core subjects of the National Curriculum. Under the heading 'Mathematics' we find:

> Sorting objects by own criteria
> Recognise number symbols
> Understand next to, under, behind, between
> Recognise and name shapes circle, square, triangle and rectangle
> Order at least four objects by size.

Under the heading 'Science', there appears:

> Makes observations of familiar materials and communicates these
> Asks how, what, why questions
> Talks about characteristics of living things
> Identifies materials metal, wood, plastic, paper, cloth and glass
> Identifies materials that are hard or soft.

Under the heading 'Language', we find:

> Asks questions
> Gives explanations
> Responds to instructions
> Listens and responds to stories

Reads pictures
Looks at books for pleasure
Reading
Names or sound letters
Uses some letter symbols
Writes own name

(The scoring chart for the above does include scoring for competence in home language as well as in English).

All the above are to be scored on a scale of 1-3 (what, in the bad old days, we used to call poor, average and above average!) There is no space on this Checklist for narrative to substantiate any of the judgements.

In the list of items chosen to be assessed one can clearly detect the cold hand of the National Curriculum Attainment Target criteria creeping in to early years assessment profiles. It is even more interesting to note what is not there. For instance in language there is nothing on children's ability to give oral accounts, personal narratives or tell imaginative stories. There is nothing on developmental writing except the bald 'uses some letter symbols'.

In mathematics there is nothing about children using symbolic representation, nothing on pattern, nothing on prediction nor investigation nor hypothesising. Nothing, either, on playing with ideas involving maths.

In science, the assessment of the development of thinking and the ability to speculate and reflect is confined solely to 'ask how, what and why questions'. In fact middle class children have been well trained in this type of questioning. Yet voicing such questions is not the only way children develop thinking skills or abstract thought. Some may ask these or similar questions silently in their heads. When we watch their experimentation in action we may get glimpses of the processes of their thinking, but there is nothing in the record on observing processes such as might occur in play.

Teaching to the test

I would question whether this type of record serves the interests of children or whether it is likely to under-represent their real achievements as learners and to restrict our view of their development. For those adults, parents or early years pre-school workers who are in the know, it will almost certainly lead to some form of teaching to the test. It serves the interests of those who want an easy method of comparing narrow achievement on entry with narrow achievements at age 7 and thus comparing school with school. In their anxiety to have something concrete and a simple way of assessing children's skills and competence on entering nursery or reception class, adults may resort to this type of list without pausing to consider whether it really tells them anything very valuable about the individual child.

My point is that the selection of items for the tick list of the Can do/can't do type is a subjective matter which might well be based on dubious criteria unrelated to the real contexts of children's learning. Children in multi-ethnic classrooms and working class children in general will be likely to be seen to be underachieving if this form of assessment is used. How ethnic minority and black and working class children have been assessed has always been a matter of concern, not least to parents, who see their children placed in lower streams or ability groups, see them underachieving in tests, and whose questions about whether this is fair go unanswered. Our knowledge is 'racialised' in favour of certain groups. This is bound to impact onto assessment. The debates about the cultural bias in the London Reading Test seem far away, but the cultural bias contained in the SATs is no less worrying.

The problem with assessment and records that pick out lists of testable items is that they limit both the teacher and the learner. They can at worst become an alternative curriculum, so that activities are planned with narrow outcomes in mind. This will tend to produce sterile learning situations and actually depress real levels of achievement.

We need to ask whether teaching to the test can really support us in building on what the child can do and understand and on what the child brings to the learning situation. Does it not rather focus our attention on what children cannot do, and on what certain groups of children cannot do, thus feeding assumptions about ethnic minority children based on deficit models of their language, culture and attitudes to child-rearing and education.

Mary Jane Drummond (1994) points to the injustice of using scales of assessment which 'are not underpinned by any representation of the process of children's learning.' She goes on to criticise such types of 'induction screening' because:

> the authors do not explain how the teachers' assessments fulfil the purpose of ensuring 'relevance of activity for individual children'. What do the teachers actually do when they have assessed some at level 5 as having excellent/good hand eye co-ordination' and some as 'poorly co-ordinated, clumsy'...

> Children have the right to be taken seriously and respectfully as learners...our assessment formats should not only teach us about learning, but should record learning that we treasure and prize (Drummond, 1994).

Assessment through observation

The SEAC pamphlet, *Assessment Matters: observation in school science* sets out guidance on the process of scientific observation which we would perhaps do well to note.

> Observation is not a process to be carried out in isolation. It forms part of whole investigations, where it serves some purpose. Though it appears straightforward it is actually a very complex process. Conceptual knowledge cannot be removed from the process of observation as it guides the selection and interpretation of the observations made.
>
> Perception of the task's purpose interacts with the knowledge and experience of the observer in deciding which features are relevant (SEAC, 1992).

If we apply this to our own observations of children as learners it becomes apparent how crucial are our understandings of the learning we are supposed to be observing and our understandings of the purpose which the observations will serve.

What to assess

The most helpful distinction in my mind between a record that is useful and one that is not is to look at whether it records learning as a process or whether it just records isolated task achievement. This is not just a question of formative versus summative assessment. Whether as parent or teacher, I find most useful and exciting those observations which tell me **how** the child learnt something, **how** the child demonstrated progress in scientific or linguistic or mathematical understanding. No tick in a box against a standardised statement will ever do this. Only a record which is an observational record with narrative comment will.

What is useful is an understanding of the kinds of things to look for, although we should be conscious that when we look we have made a choice based on a conceptual framework. This conceptual framework needs to be spelt out, not least so that it can be constantly rescrutinised. This is particularly important in a multicultural context. In deciding what features are relevant we are making cultural choices. An obvious example is the observation of children's linguistic competence. We decide whether to observe and include children's linguistic competence in their community languages. If we decide not to include it that decision will have an immediate effect on what we choose to observe and how we choose to interpret our observations. Observing a bilingual child who is silent in a group situation, we could simply record that the child 'had no language'. Or we could observe that 'in group interactions in English the child listens attentively and by joining in the activity is beginning to demonstrate understanding of English. Mother reports that in group situations at home, the child is very competent at expressing her wishes and observations in Turkish and asks endless questions when they go out shopping'.

When a child is observed who 'cannot name colours and shapes of objects correctly', we are making a decisions that **naming** colours or shapes is important. Is it? Why? Parents in white English culture tend to teach the words for colours early on. Much pre-school adult-child talk tends to focus on this. 'What a nice jumper/coat. What colour is it?' Is it equally valued behaviour in all cultures? The mathematical concept is to be able to discriminate between objects based on colour, shape and size. This does not necessarily involve naming at all. If we were to contextualise this in observing play, would a child habitually choose the red car which has a friction motor or the blue car which does not?

Selective Assessment

In the baseline assessment records/checklists I have seen, I am struck with the way that a very small number of behaviours have been selected and promoted in significance by placing them in a baseline assessment record. So what? you may say. But the consequences of this can possibly be quite damaging, particularly when dealing with children from a wide variety of social and cultural backgrounds. Because the selection process itself is biased from the start. And that means that the judgement it prompts adults to make will be similarly biased from the start. We need to remind ourselves of all the research from the 1960s to the present that has shown the damaging effect on black and ethnic minority and working class children and girls of stereotyped or low teacher expectations (See, *inter alia* Rist, 1970, Rosenthal and Jacobson, 1968, Davie, Butler and Goldstein, 1972, Clarricoates, 1980, Tomlinson, 1980, Mac an Ghaill, 1988). Can we be certain that our assessment practices in the early years are not contributing to maintaining stereotyped expectations?

Conclusion

Fortunately, early years workers themselves are daily making many more and varied observations of their children than they will record on these mechanistic forms. They will know the children as individual learners. They will talk excitedly to parents and to each other about a particular achievement or process of learning. Much of the richness of their daily observations is never written down. However it is important that sometimes it is. It is also important that parents have the opportunity to write things down about their children, as in Sheila Wolfendale's record, *All About Me,* which parents complete.

If we do not have a written record that has 'proper respect for children's minds, for their power to think, to create, to imagine, to explore, to reason, to puzzle, to wonder and dream' (Drummond, 1992) and one which is able adequately to document the diversity of their learning in different social and cultural contexts and with different pedagogical and cultural content, what we are left with, or what we will have imposed on us, are the reductionist and constricting models of assessment represented by many of the burgeoning Baseline checklists. Children will be labelled according to what is written down and not on the basis of what we really know about them. Therefore if what is written misrepresents or under-represents children's achievements and the really interesting pattern of their progress in learning, we will have failed our children.

Chapter 5

Assessment of bilingual pupils: issues of fluency

Maggie Gravelle and Elaine Sturman

The School Assessment Folder for 1993 included a section which considers National Curriculum assessment with particular reference to bilingual pupils, indicating a recognition of teachers' concerns and a willingness to acknowledge and legitimise their views. Many of the points encourage discussion. Some of the positive ideas will support teachers in providing appropriate learning experiences for their bilingual pupils.

Unlike in previous years, the 1994 School Assessment Folder for Key Stage 1 only supersedes the 1993 version where there have been specific changes to the assessment arrangements. The section on fluency in the 1993 School Assessment Folder is therefore still current at time of writing and represents the latest SCAA advice on support for bilingual pupils.

In contrast to much of the rest of the School Assessment Folder, the section on the assessment of bilingual pupils does not seem to represent a clear position on the part of its compilers. It reads more as though it were a compilation of a range of different responses to the 1991/2 SATs. Because of this each paragraph should be considered independently and as a starting point for debate and discussion. Critical reading could lead to the development of practical strategies in schools but the document itself provides no examples or solutions.

The School Assessment Folder does take one step forward, in that it makes bilingual pupils visible. It does so by recognising their presence in the majority of our schools and by acknowledging the language skills that they bring into the classroom. It highlights the need for all teachers to 'develop a systematic approach to teaching, learning and assessment'. Thus the responsibility for the learning and achievement of bilingual pupils rests with the class teacher. Some suggestions for implementing a systematic approach are given later in the section:

> any approach which ensures the children understand clearly what they have to do, and what kind of response is expected (stopping short of providing the answer or response itself) is to be encouraged;
> presenting the task in a multicultural (or multilingual) context is often beneficial;
> understanding children's responses often requires knowledge of individual children and their particular ways of expressing themselves, including non-verbal responses;
> except in the National Curriculum subject of English, there is no general requirement for children to express their knowledge and understanding solely in English;
> peer-group support may assist shy children who may hesitate while expressing responses in their first language (B6.3).

> all subjects at this key stage contain common elements of language. Activities in the classroom break down into describing, sequencing and decision making. Reading and writing break down into acquiring, categorising and using knowledge; establishing the relationships between things; and judging what counts as good or bad, or the reasons for following a course of action. It may well be that simple structures of this kind will be of particular help to second language learners to understand what they are being introduced to, and by implication what they are being expected to demonstrate for the purposes of assessment (B6.5).

Such strategies are supportive for all pupils, not only bilingual learners. When teachers analyse the demands of tasks and develop related activities they are attempting to explicate the learning. It is a matter of clarification not simplification. The School Assessment Folder implies that the 'common elements of language' which it identifies constitutes a complete list. Not only is it incomplete but also, as an abstract list it does not go far enough. Elements such as sequencing and categorising are helpful but need to be developed as the basis for practical activities.

Sequencing: Tasks such as recording experiments, giving instructions, recounting events or writing a story all involve sequencing. Pupils can be given a model, asked to put sections of a text (their own or a given text) in order or be given some sections and asked to supply the missing parts.

Categorising: Scientific properties, personal responses (true/false, good/bad) and ways of handling data may all involve categorisation. Pupils can be asked to make charts, carry out and tabulate responses to surveys or sort objects or statements.

Reading and writing: It is obviously important to think about language structures. Pattern and repetition of language will help all children to engage with a text and will enhance bilingual children's understanding. Texts should be checked for idiomatic use of English which may be unfamiliar and hinder understanding. It is also important to consider the content of reading material. Picture and context cues should relate to the text in a meaningful way. This is more important than trying to select texts using a notion of 'cultural familiarity'. Bilingual learners need to be offered the full range of literature; fiction and non-fiction, realism and fantasy, challenging and easy, familiar and unfamiliar. They should not be confined to books which are stereotypically deemed to be suitable for them.

Giving children a rich choice of material will support them in their own writing by providing a wide range of models. In writing, placing undue emphasis on 'correct spelling and grammar' will inhibit, in particular, developing bilinguals' imaginative and linguistic creativity.

It is most important to provide a range of collaborative activities in which talk is essential to learning.

> Bilingual children, whether they are fluent in English or not, have abilities and achievements in their home language which can and should be recognised and celebrated by schools (B6.2).

This is certainly true. The question remains how it is to be achieved. There have always been a number of dangers in attempts to 'recognise and celebrate' home language and culture. Teachers must be careful not to make assumptions about children's experiences of language, religion, home life etc. Mistaken assumptions can all too easily lead teachers into giving inappropriate information about particular life-styles. This is misleading for all pupils and especially damaging for those who are being misrepresented. It does not celebrate their abilities and achievements. Equally, singling out pupils and expecting them to act as representatives of a whole culture or way of life can hinder their learning.

Culture is not, in any case, a homogeneous concept. Tokenistic references — for example including one Asian name, passing references to Carnival or introducing a single Islamic patterned border — can appear to children as a failure to take their backgrounds seriously.

Children need to know that their language and culture is accepted and that their experiences are relevant and can be used to help learning. We would challenge the view that 'conflicting demands placed upon these children may affect their learning ability ...and rate of progress' B6.8. This stems from a middle class, Eurocentric perception that if the culture of the home and the school are different, this will prevent children from learning. As long as children are encouraged to treat their own experiences as equally valid this conflict should not arise.

In assessment, we should be acknowledging the language skills which bilinguals use automatically, for example the ability to use their languages appropriately and without becoming confused. The cognitive advantages of being bilingual should be made explicit to parents and children as well as to teachers. Even at the early stages of developing English, bilingual learners can reflect on the diversity of their language use, on the situations in which they speak in different languages and on the similarities and differences between their languages. It is easier for the bilingual children who are more fluent in English to appreciate and enjoy the subtleties of language and to accept and be interested in languages which they do not understand.

The School Assessment Folder attempts to be positive but it has not eliminated deficit views. Would statements such as: 'Not all these children will necessarily be fluent in their home language' be made about monolingual children? One assumption behind such a statement is that bilingualism is a problem not only for the teacher but for the children themselves. It suggests that language development in the homes of bilingual pupils is different from and inferior to that in monolingual, English speaking homes. Another assumption is that learning in two languages will result in neither language being acquired properly.

In the School Assessment Folder, fluency is often used to mean fluency in English. It suggests that it is possible to identify three or four stages of English language development 'quite precisely'. Even if it were possible to do so the time spent in assigning stages to children could be better used. Language acquisition is not a linear process. So it does not necessarily depend on the length of time children have 'been within a second language learning environment' (B6.4). The context in which language is used will make a difference to the stage at which the child seems to be operating. It is far more useful to observe what children do in different contexts and situations in order to make decisions about how to support their language development, than simply to describe their stage.

The notion of progress in fluency is based on misconceptions about the acquisition of English. Children will develop English fluency when:

• they hear it used in real situations

• their understanding is supported by real objects, pictures, gestures etc.

• conceptual development is encouraged through English and any other languages in which they feel confident

• they are encouraged to use all their language skills in the learning situation

• they are presented with situations in which they need and want to communicate in English

• they feel valued and able to take risks

• they perceive a positive attitude towards their bilingualism. Even monolingual teachers can recognise and use the language diversity within and beyond the classroom by exploiting their own abilities in accent, dialect and any other languages.

Personality is more significant than general learning ability in the development of fluency. Factors such as motivation, confidence, 'extrovertness', stress and sensitivity will have an effect. Teachers should strive to create an environment which gives children time, space and understanding. They must not conclude that children lack 'fluency', when what they might lack is confidence.

The tone of NCC and SEAC advice has been to suggest that lower scores for bilingual children are only to be expected and that they give teachers an indication of need. Such low scores, however, could affect the expectations of parents, teachers and children. Most attention needs to be paid to explaining the limitations of end of Key Stage assessment to parents, because these assessments are not likely to indicate accurately a child's level of knowledge and understanding. Unfortunately, these assessments are likely to impinge on the next level of tests, and ultimately on allocations to examination tiers or bands. The way the whole assessment system operates is bound to discriminate against bilingual learners but it is the system that is at fault, not the children. The procedures do not allow bilingual learners to demonstrate their strengths and may well be testing them on areas of weakness. Even schools that would like to provide the opportunity which the assessment process allows (e.g. use of first language in Maths and Science and a wide interpretation of how understanding may be conveyed) do not have the resources to do so. As the School Assessment Folder recognises, it is not enough just to offer additional support for SATs:

> The provision of additional resources such as home language adult support should be made as part of the whole school development plan on a consistent basis;

> providing such support on an exceptional basis, during the standard assessment task period only for example, is not likely to be helpful to children who are not accustomed to such help (B6.2).

Increasingly, SATs are becoming an assessment of product rather than process. Teacher assessment is recognised as allowing teachers to become more aware of the range of pupils' experience and attainment 'by consolidating them within the records of achievement process, and by extending the range of learning experiences and opportunities' (B6.5). This would be admirable were it not for the emphasis on league tables which work against this broad view of learning and achievement. The School Assessment Folder recognises the power that teachers have to affect learning and assess achievement. Schools could consider making this a priority within the IDP. The guidance to heads and teachers (B6.7 and 6.8) could be used to support this, provided it was also backed up with time and other resources.

It is encouraging that the School Assessment Folder gives useful strategies for the realistic assessment of bilingual learners. We hope that teachers will build on this to start to redress the balance for the benefit of bilingual children. Concentrating on Teacher Assessment will continue this process and enhance teachers' professional status.

Many of our schools, and not only these in the inner cities have pupils who speak languages other than English. We have argued that curriculum provision and assessment must take their needs and abilities into account. In his report *The National Curriculum and its Assessment,* Ron Dearing scarcely even acknowledges the existence of cultural and linguistic diversity, although we cannot be the only people who responded to his pleas and expressed our views — receiving a friendly acknowledgement.

He recommends (para. 5.20) that all students should study a foreign language at Key Stage 4, largely for reasons of economic prosperity and trade. Yet he fails to recognise the importance of extending and building on children's existing language skills throughout their school years.

The majority of NCC and SEAC documents have made it clear that bilingualism is not and should not be regarded as a special educational need. It is worrying that the Dearing report fails to do so. It therefore leaves the opportunity for misunderstanding and consequent low expectations, particularly in the light of the recommendation (para 6.4ii) that pupils who are 'working below the current prescribed ranges...continue to work at the level appropriate to them...'

The next two years will be crucial if, as the report promises, we are to have a subsequent period of stability. Those who are concerned with the teaching and assessment of bilingual learners will have to maintain both vigilance and pressure if their needs are not to be totally ignored.

Chapter 6

Assessing primary progress

Elaine Sturman and Martin Francis

The declared intention of the National Curriculum is to give all children in maintained schools the entitlement to a broad and balanced curriculum — a worthy intention notwithstanding the difficulties of deciding what its content might be. For parents and children who have been discriminated against because of teachers' low expectations, the National Curriculum could be welcomed as an attempt to ensure that they are no longer offered a diminished curriculum. However 'offering' a curriculum does not in itself ensure equal access to it.

There has been an official assumption that by merely prescribing what should be taught, learning will take place and standards be raised. However it is not a matter of feeding children dollops of content but of teachers deciding how to manage the learning process. How to break down the content for instance, or how to make content accessible, how to relate it to the child's own experience, how the child's motivation might be affected by class, race or gender bias in the content. The teacher needs then to think about the best way to organise the teaching of this content: the balance between individual, group or whole class organisation; the composition of groups related to particular tasks; the type of work that takes place within the group — for example co-operation on a single task or differentiated individual efforts towards a shared outcome; the differentiation of task and/or outcome.

Finally the teacher will have to decide how the content will be recorded and assessed: how to match different forms of recording to content *and* pupils; what to assess and how to do it. For example in a task involving the composition of a piece of music, the teacher could assess the final performance; the process of composition with a group or the method children devised to record their composition; communication skills within the group; the allocation of tasks within the group; individual contributions to managing the task. The teacher needs also to evaluate all the decisions made about content, organisation and assessment, in order to see whether s/he was successful in matching pupil, content, method and task. We must remember that we are not only assessing the child as learner but also ourselves as teachers. Of course this is what the Government wants to do but in a much more simplistic way. In fact we in return can assess the adequacy of the Government's prescriptive ideas about content.

Some of these considerations might seem unimportant because they are not incorporated in the National Curriculum Documents but, if they are not taken into account, the recording of *progress* through the National Curriculum will be impossible. This was acknowledged by SEAC when they stressed the importance of recording achievement wider than the National Curriculum SoAs, and has been endorsed in the Dearing recommendations.

Assessment in context

It is important to remember that the 'Statements of Attainment' in the unrevised National Curriculum are fallible statements made up by a group of people. They do not necessarily reflect the ways individual children learn nor the sequence in which they learn. There is a danger that the 'level descriptors' proposed by Dearing to replace the SoAs will fall into the same trap. Similarly, the examples given in SAT guidance for teachers are not the only ways to prove that a child has reached a particular stage of development and indeed might not in themselves prove anything. When making their own teacher assessments and interpreting performance in tests, teachers must retain the right to make their own professional judgements based on their knowledge of children and the learning process.

This is particularly important when we look at assessment in terms of class, ethnicity, bilingualism and gender. The knowledge and experience children bring to school will vary according to their background — their stock of 'cultural capital' will account for some of the ways in which they interpret tasks and communicate their thoughts. Many of the tasks in the first SATs required children to explain, discuss, hypothesise — all language-based skills which can easily favour the middle class native standard-English speaker over the working class or bilingual pupil. Of course this need not be the case but the teacher has to be aware of the different ways in which an explanation could be framed. The teacher's knowledge of language repertoires and the different types of experience that inform them will be greatly enhanced if she works in a school where this knowledge and experience is valued and taken into account when the curriculum is planned.

If we concentrate too much on looking for the 'correct' explanations we can easily miss the child who comes at the problem from an unusual angle. Additionally, by looking for the verbal evidence we risk overlooking other ways in which a child is demonstrating understanding or knowledge. For example the Technology National Curriculum seeks evidence of children's ability to perceive a need and plan a project to answer that need. A child may well demonstrate a form of concrete planning through manipulating materials, testing their strength or flexibility, comparing one material with another, doing it all manually without any verbalisation, but clearly thinking it through so that the 'plan' forms itself in her mind. That nothing is written or drawn on paper nor verbalised does not mean that 'planning' has not taken place.

Enriching assessment opportunities

When bilingual children in the early stages of learning English are assessed without the aid of an interpreter, explanations need to be very carefully given and monitored, so that we do not penalise them for their lack of understanding of English. We asked a child how we could test whether plants needed light to enable them to grow and she answered that we could close the windows. In later discussions we established that we should have interpreted this as 'draw the curtains'. Children need to be given the chance to 'show' what they would do to establish something in science or technology, rather than just to 'tell' us. This applies as much to those working class pupils who are less comfortable with the school's language repertoire as it does to bilingual children.

It is clear that process-based activities are more likely than pencil and paper tests to extend children's opportunities to demonstrate what they know and what they can do. Despite all our misgivings about the time they took, some of the first reported SATs, in particular Science AT1 (floating and sinking) and Maths AT1 (devising a maths game), provided a richer basis for assessment. We need to make sure that our teacher assessments provide similar opportunities. One way to do this is to look at the skills that, although expressed in different terminology, are common to all or most National Curriculum areas and to base teacher assessment upon them. We can observe children carrying out activities and observe the processes at work, by what they say to each other and the teacher, their response to the group, and also by what they actually do. We all know children who can explain what they are about to do, but then have trouble doing it, because they cannot translate the theory into practice or lack the manual dexterity. Adults might well be able to tell you what they think makes a good 'Whodunit?' but not be able to write one, or be able to repair a car engine but not to *tell* you how the internal combustion engine works.

If we don't provide activities with rich potential assessment opportunities we won't be able to make full and fair assessments of the children. We should be devising activities that show us *how* the children learn, as well as *what* they have learnt. We need to take account of their knowledge and experience and to make sure that the content we provide enables them to build on this and use it to enhance learning. We must also find ways of making the content accessible. This is particularly important with bilingual learners new to English. They will need support for understanding, which is often best provided by working collaboratively with more fluent English speakers. The example of activities that follow were designed to fulfil these conditions through the study of a text, *Zeynep: that really happened to me.* We have deliberately chosen work which was initiated before the National Curriculum took place, to show that it is still possible to undertake work of this kind and fulfil National Curriculum requirements. At the time of writing this work covered English AT1 and AT2, History AT1 and AT2, Geography AT2 and AT4 and the cross-curricular theme of Economic Understanding.

Activity-based assessment — a case study

Zeynep is the true story of a deportation case in Hackney, told by Zeynep and her teacher. When the Hasbudak family was threatened with deportation the children, Zeynep and Fatih, were both at William Patten Infant School. Parents, children and teachers from the school campaigned to reverse the deportation order. The story of the campaign, as told in the book, establishes a role of the school as part of the wider community and shows that political issues cannot be ignored when they affect the lives of children and their families.

Unlike many of the books produced for young children, *Zeynep* is a true story. It has many of the elements of good fiction — build-up and release of tension; an identified villain; celebration and sadness; friendship and mutual support — but no happy ending nor the cathartic effect of fictional tragedy. Despite all the school's efforts, the Hasbudak family was deported.

Zeynep was chosen as a teaching resource because of its relevance to children's own lives and its powerful potential for engaging their emotions. Choice of material, the structure of the activities devised and the composition of the groups who work on them all make an important contribution to the effectiveness of learning. The children must be able to engage with the material in a group. The group must be supportive and allow everyone opportunity to participate through activities which really call for collaboration.

Activities

1. Time-line to record the events in Zeyep's life as described in the book

This demands close examination of the text to identify and sequence the events. It also enables children to think about the future, predicting the next part of Zeynep's story and making their own choices about what might happen to her. As well as providing opportunities for creative writing, this can also alleviate some of the potentially negative feelings brought about by the ending of the book.

The teacher selected significant events from the text and wrote them on individual cards. The children could refer to the book for visual support if a word on the cards caused difficulty. The teacher asked the children to sequence the cards in a logical order. Some of the events had a fixed point on the time-line (eg 'born in London', 'starts school') whilst others were open to interpretation, giving room for negotiation within the group (eg 'party at school'). Once the cards were sequenced to the satisfaction of the group illustrations were added, allowing the activity to be revisited and reinforced.

This activity could have been extended in a number of ways:

a. *What might have happened to Zeynep since the end of the story?* Having established the pattern of describing and sequencing events, the children could use the same pattern to predict the next events in Zeynep's life and record them on the time-line. The time-line could become the basis for a more extended piece of writing — a narrative modelled on the original Zeynep text or a letter from Zeynep describing her experiences.

b. *Time-line for Fatih, Zeynep's brother.* The children could decide for themselves which events to include from the text and predict future events for Fatih.

c. *Individual time-lines.* After these activities the children would be in a much better position to make their own time-lines. They would be familiar with the demands of time-line activities and have a model based on someone else's experience before embarking on the sensitive process of constructing their own.

2. Campaigning

Examples of campaigning occur and recur throughout the story. Examining them helped the children to become familiar with the idea of campaigning, both as portrayed in the book and also as applied to other issues. The teacher wanted to link information from the book with children's own knowledge of other campaigns.

The teacher identified campaigning methods from the text and wrote them on green cards: letter writing, collecting signatures, making banners, demonstrating, voting, having meetings, getting publicity, raising money.

Next, she selected small sections from the text (phrases and sentences, speech and narrative) to exemplify the campaigning methods and wrote them on blue cards.

The children matched the blue cards with the green. In some cases correspondence was obvious, while others exemplified more than one method so that placing them needed negotiation. Because blue and green cards did not match one to one, the task was at once more flexible and more demanding.

The format meant that children had to work at making sense of the text. Copies of the book were always available so the children could reflect on the text, note and respond to one another's ideas, and return to the matching activity whenever they felt like it. There was no single 'right' answer.

The children also drew pictures about the campaigning methods. This was another ongoing activity which provided extra visual support for their reading.

Children working on tasks of this kind will talk together to sort out their own ideas and help each other negotiate the learning. For bilingual learners the peer group provides the highest motivation for language development and ensures that they hear models of everyday speech.

Children who are new to English need to be given access to the task, to hear appropriate language patterns and vocabulary being repeated and to have support with reading. Working with others who are more competent in English will be helpful, as long as every child is able to make a contribution.

Although children often work best in friendship groups there needs to be an understanding in the classroom that they will be expected to work in other groupings at times. Working in friendship groups can lead to situations where

74

some children are excluded or where children become so used to working together that they no longer challenge each other. Once a pecking order is established it can be very hard to break.

Holistic Assessment

The School Assessment Folders Key Stage One in both 1993 and 1994 promoted a wide view of acceptable evidence for teacher assessment. They interpret 'written work' as including charts and diagrams as well as structured pieces of writing; they encourage teachers to credit children with any response that *conveys* understanding. They discuss different forms of support children might be given and accept evidence in the mother tongue for Maths and Science. Furthermore they state that this should be part of normal classroom practice, not a special provision for end of key stage assessment. They also value teachers' notes and observations as important evidence. We support this broader definition of what counts as evidence, including the use of photographs of completed work and work in progress and tapes and videos made by teachers and children.

Much of the assessment of collaborative work will be by observation. Teachers need to assess the effectiveness of the group as a whole and the role of individuals within it. They will have to respond flexibly to what they observe by trying different groupings and knowing when to intervene to confirm a child's understanding and when to move on. They will also be assessing the suitability of the task and their own introduction, structuring and resourcing and may need to change what they do in the light of what they find.

When planning the children's work, teachers should have some idea of the assessment opportunities that might arise. Teachers should aim to 'build in ' a range of different forms of assessment over the year, to give opportunities for all the different learning processes children use to be integrated into their overall assessment. Assessment methods should therefore include observation and listening in order to record that the child's questioning and responding; the individual's participation in the group; and interaction including facilitating, initiating and responding.

Asking children questions about what they are doing before, during or after an activity will provide additional assessment information. Teachers need to monitor their own question technique carefully, as it is all too easy for children to think that a 'correct' response is expected, even if and when the teacher has no preconceptions about the answer. Encouraging children to present their work to the class or group enables teachers to assess presentation and the understanding demonstrated.

It is simplistic to respond to government strictures merely by saying 'we assess children all the time' or 'the test doesn't tell us anything we didn't know already'. We have to make a convincing professional argument, demonstrating how much more sophisticated our own forms of assessment are. Ongoing assessment must allow our own provision (level of resourcing, appropriateness of materials, groupings, suitability of teaching and learning styles, accessibility of content) to be part of what is assessed, thus contributing to the development of more effective teaching throughout the school. We are moving away from the limitations of individual pupil assessment to what could be termed 'whole school assessment'. Carried out rigorously, systematically and with a willingness to be self-critical and challenge shibboleths, assessment of this kind will provide a powerful foundation for the teaching profession's challenge to centralised control of the education system and the de-skilling of the teaching profession.

Chapter 7

The Role of Black Parents in Schools

Patsy Daniels

Black people's experience of the education system is all to often of being treated as unintelligent. Such experience has inhibited many black children's achievement. Some schools still tend to push black children into sport and not help them to achieve in the academic areas of school life. The entitlement ensured for every child to the National Curriculum by the Education Reform Act of 1988 should, in theory, put an end to these procedures.

In the 1950s and '60s, black parents left the formal teaching of their children in the hands of professionals. Then as the years went by they found that their children were not attaining as highly as they had expected. Many, in fact, were being labelled 'educationally subnormal' (Coard, 1971). By the early '70s black parents had set up their own Saturday schools in an attempt to help their children where the British education system failed.

A report for a London borough, *Race Issues and the Development of the Education Services* (1990) makes several pertinent points. The report found widespread dissatisfaction with the education system amongst ethnic minority communities. Many parents were concerned about what they saw as lack of discipline, failure to teach basic skills and an unstructured approach to their children's learning. Parents believed that local schools had low expectations of their children. Some parents were told that their children were 'doing well' but then found them entered for the bottom GCSE levels. At a local supplementary school for African Caribbean pupils, the teachers found themselves explaining and re-explaining tasks set by schools, because the children had not had the confidence to ask teachers for help.

The process of pupil alienation seems to start in the primary school. If black children are inquisitive and lively some white teachers seemed to react negatively. Instead of encouraging pupils and channelling their curiosity, they can frustrate them by ignoring their questions or react to their exuberance as if it were indiscipline. Cecile Wright (1992) documents the case of Marcus, eager to answer the teacher's questions but always ignored by her, until he becomes restless. Where upon the teacher suddenly notices him and says: 'Sit down, Marcus and stop fidgeting'. Teachers and other adults in the classroom were seen to behave in less than acceptable ways. The report records cases of teachers anglicising children's names for their own convenience, sighing or rolling their eyes when children could not carry out instructions because they did not understand them, and making slighting comments in the staffroom about the competence or commitment of parents.

One African Caribbean teacher who had worked with black girls found them to be alienated by the European-orientated curriculum. No mention was made in English classes of black writers, nor did the girls know that black scientists or inventors existed, before she told them. They knew little about the Caribbean and nothing about African languages and achievements.

This report was written over 20 years after issues of this kind first caused concern. Black parents are finding that attitudes have still not changed. Yet black parents have the same rights as white parents. It is vital that their views are reflected on governing bodies through adequate representation. With proper information and support, they can be suitably armed for the significant role that governors must now play.

Local Management of Schools and the Role of Governors

The 1986 Education Act made important changes to the way schools are managed. Under Local Management of Schools (LMS) the revised composition and duties of governing bodies have important implications for black parents and their children. It is the new responsibilities of governors that is most significant.

Governors are responsible by law for:

- all the school's finances — LEAs are now required to delegate budgets to all schools with more than 200 pupils
- policies on the delivery of the National Curriculum, including policies on religious and sex education
- policy on discipline and exclusions
- special needs provision
- complaints from parents
- the annual report to parents
- links with local communities
- the appointment, discipline and promotion of teachers
- health and safety and building maintenance at the school.

The day to day running of the school is still the responsibility of the headteacher. Governors and headteachers have direct control of the running of the school and the deployment of resources for the school's own education needs and priorities. They decide the salaries of the staff, the running costs including the budget for books and equipment. They decide how the curriculum is to be delivered, and about matters concerning individual pupils and their parents.

Parent governors are generally people from the community who have a genuine interest in their local school and their child's education, and they come from all walks of life.

Although unpaid, they are expected to take on huge responsibilities, have varied areas of understanding and expertise, and do a good deal of work. It is unlikely that every member of a governing body is able to take up this voluntary work to the same degree, and therefore those who can afford more involvement will probably have greater influence.

Governing bodies now have more parent governors and fewer LEA representatives, and this has increased the potential influence of parents as a whole. The idea behind this is the notion that 'parents are the consumers so they should have the say. If you have a child at the school, you can become a parent governor by being elected by the other parents. Or you could become a co-opted governor if the governing body appoints you as a representative of a community, or for any important contribution you might offer. Teacher governors represent teachers at the school, and there are 'minor authority' governors appointed by the local council or LEA. Headteachers can be governors if they choose to do so.

Black Governors

Across the country, few black parents have been on school governing bodies in the past, and even today with the new arrangements there are disproportionately few. This is especially true of African Caribbean parents. The Department of Education and Science found in a survey (Keys and Fernades, 1990) that just over 1% of governors were from ethnic minority groups. Other surveys (CDF, 1990; CRE, 1993; and NFER, 1993) all found representation through black governors to be disproportionately low (quoted in Bagley, 1993).

Some black parents, deeply concerned for their children's education, have tried to become governors, but many lack confidence in the area of education. In my experience, many have felt isolated and unwelcome on governing bodies. They have not felt valued and have tended to be excluded from membership of some of the key sub-committees such as finance.

Bagley's study raises crucial issues about the recruitment, training and support of black governors. A root concern is the matter of training for all governors in equal opportunities and race issues. His survey suggests a gloomy prospect of diminishing interest from governors in taking up such specific training because of general lack of awareness as well as financial constraints. The possibilities for LEAs to lead in this area have been limited. Without governors themselves actively seeking to increase black representation so that the school's pupil population is reflected, there is usually little prospect of parents in a predominantly white school electing black parent governors.

Experience in some LEAs covered in Bagley's study indicates that a range of sustained strategies is required to recruit more black governors. One strategy must tackle getting information through successfully to community groups. It has to be done sensitively, as communities are often suspicious after past dealings with officials. Communications should for example be offered in community languages. There must also be adequate training and maintained support for the people who are recruited. The role of a lone black governor is difficult, yet it holds the key to recruiting others.

Most governing bodies have established subcommittees to deal with the volume of work and to assist with the decision-making process. Governors' meetings can be rather formal occasions and this can be inhibiting for lay governors. A greater level of participation may come through training and increasing confidence. Every governor should seek to be involved in making crucial decisions.

Black governors and other lay governors may be reluctant to join in discussion of curriculum matters. Given that the curriculum is central to all children's education, every effort should be made to help black governors attain a reasonable level of understanding through training, information and networking with support groups. Judging by the NFER study on governor training, much needs to be done to provide appropriate and adequate training and to encourage its take-up. Self-help groups for black governors have been set up, aimed at boosting self-confidence, and offering mutual support. There is insufficient central support for them generally, although a few LEAs have targeted funds such as the Urban Programme towards increasing participation of minority groups in governing bodies.

The onus is now upon black parents to ask for and to attend seminars, conferences and other training programmes offered by black governors groups. This will help enable them to join the governing bodies of their children's schools. Once there, they should get themselves elected to the committees on which they feel confident about making an input e.g. finance, exclusions or curriculum. This will give black parents as a whole a greater say in what happens in their school.

Similarly, it is vital for black parents and governors to put aside divisive communal politics and to support one another. For governors to be effective, they must become well-informed. Practical information is regularly carried in the *Times Educational Supplement,* e.g. in 'Agenda' by Joan Sallis, and most public libraries take it. Black governors need to widen their representation on organisations such as the National Association of Governors and Managers (NAGM) and the National Confederation of Parents and Teachers Association (NCPTA). Unfortunately, NAGM currently represents less than a fifth of the estimated 340,000 governors in the country (TES 14.1. 1994, p.18; TES 11.2.1994, p.7), and a more nationally representative body is needed for this singularly important group of people.

Black governors should be participating via national bodies in the working groups responsible for writing the National Curriculum and tests, to ensure that together these are sensitive to needs of black children. However, it is probable that their voice has been overlooked, given that in setting up the working groups, SCAA failed to include any representation of parent groups (TES 21. 1. 1994 p.16).

Enrolment, Exclusions and SEN

Many black parents welcomed the National Curriculum and every child's entitlement to it. They had experience of their children being taught in lower streams or bands because a school or teacher assumed that they were incapable of following the same levels of study as the other children (Wright, 1986).

A few schools are now opting out of LEA control and going grant- maintained. My experience of one such school is that it has become very selective in its intake, weeding out black pupils and low achievers through increased exclusion, especially of black boys. There is little to prevent this becoming common practice. By such practice will the pattern of 'black underachievement' be finally institutionalised as a perpetual vicious circle? Black pupils do poorly because of negative attitudes to them in school — black pupils and their parents have no 'choice' but to resort to the least attractive, least resourced schools. Black parents and governors must be vigilant and actively oppose enrolment processes that select against black pupils.

The multi-layered process of exclusion also needs to be understood by black parents and they should be better supported by LEAs when their child is subject to the process. A disturbing trend shows black boys as figuring disproportionately highly in exclusion rates in schools across the country [Bourne *et. al.*, 1994]. Governors play significant roles in the decisions on permanent exclusion — another good reason for having more black governors. Until black children have adequate support at hearings for exclusion, they will continue to figure highly in exclusion rates.

Curriculum and Assessment Concerns

Although entitlement to the National Curriculum is guaranteed to all children in maintained schools in England and Wales and their progress checked against attainment targets at every stage, there are many inadequacies in the National Curriculum about which black parents have expressed concern (eg McNeil, 1987) and these are explored further in other chapters here.

For example, there are many languages spoken in our communities. Yet, as we saw in Chapter 3, the National Curriculum arrangements tend to treat French, German and Spanish as more important than the main languages from the Indian sub-continent and Africa. A largely Anglocentric perspective informs the history curriculum. What are we saying to our children, in this multicultural society? Did not black people exist before slavery? Were they not Kings and Queens? Were there not ancient African, Asian and Chinese civilisations which contributed hugely to the development of western culture and learning? Why are these aspects of history not important to all our children? Why is the Peter's Projection map, which reflects more accurately comparisons of areas by size, not widely used, and compared with Mercator and other projections? Instead, when our children are taught about Africa and the Asian subcontinent they learn mainly about the regions' poverty but not the reasons for it.

As governors, black parents can ensure that questions about eurocentricism and racial bias in the curriculum are raised at governors' meetings. It is reasonable to expect all governors and professionals to be sympathetic to the principle of factual accuracy and objective fairness in the curriculum. No one wants their children to be misinformed or misled. Awareness also needs to be raised about aspects of the hidden curriculum, such as school meals and school dress, which can operate to discriminate against or problematise black children.

Challenging though it may be, black parents must also familiarise themselves with the processes of assessment and acquire some understanding of the issues that underlie it. Familiarity with the National Curriculum and its assessment system will be essential if they are to play their full expected and statutory role. This book discusses current issues to do with assessment and black children. Parents can also obtain documents direct from the DFE and SCAA, or read them in the local library. Black parents should take note of special arrangements that are allowed by SCAA, and which their child may need.

Following the Dearing Report in January 1994 schools will be receiving new definitions of the subjects of the National Curriculum and their assessment by Standard Assessment Tasks and teacher assessments by the end of the year. Parents should be involved in the debates leading to these definitions, especially during the consultation months (May-July, 1994). Moreover, parents should note that the contentious issue of publishing league tables of school results and truancy rates, which is known to unfairly disadvantage many schools, is still strongly supported by the government. They say that such information is needed for 'accountability to parents and society'. Parents must enter this debate and speak for themselves.

Little is said outside the teaching profession about teaching and learning styles. Yet in planning both learning and assessment, account should be taken of the different preferred learning styles of individual children. Governors should be asking questions about the range of activities offered to children in delivering subject areas, and how pupils are being prepared for assessment in terms of knowledge, skills and understanding.

One of the most important things that black governors can do is to encourage schools to devise a policy which, among much else, includes aims and details of how the school intends to manage assessment for pupils as individuals. The assessment being implemented needs to have credibility. It must be seen by all pupils to have some purpose. When a child sees the point of what he or she is doing, motivation is likely to be much higher. Rehana Minhas explores this further on page 94.

This and many other aspects are part of OFSTED inspections, something in which parents are also involved. When inspecting a school, OFSTED inspectors must hold a meeting with parents and record their views (see also Chapter 8). Here is an important opportunity for black parents, along with others, to voice their concerns. Schools are obliged to offer regular feedback to parents, in accordance with the DFE Circular 14/92 (Reports on Individual Pupils' Achievements). Another role that black parents and governors could assume is to ensure that black parents are given reports on their children and information about the school in terms and in the languages which they find accessible. Information explaining the new curriculum and assessment procedures can be communicated by leaflets and newsletters and if necessary orally.

Ealing LEA has produced a booklet, *Parents and Teachers Working Together,* which sets out the parents' role in supporting their children's learning. They note that parents are children's first teachers, teaching them to recognise colours, parts of their bodies and their names, and, among much else, the difference between right and wrong. They suggest that parents should always promote a positive image of the school and encourage their children to do their best at school.

The booklet continues by supplying detailed advice on how parents can support their children's education — by, for instance, discussing with them the television programmes they watch, taking them to the library, museums etc., involving them in the household chores such as shopping and cooking, listening to them read, praising and encouraging them and above all talking to them about their school day.

In one authority some schools have begun a paid 'parents organiser' scheme (see TES 11.2.94 p.2). This is effectively raising parental involvement in schools. When black parents do become more regularly involved in the school, they are more likely to become governors. In so doing they will be exercising their right in achieving the best for all pupils, while also looking specifically at issues concerning black pupils in education.

Glossary of Terms relating to Governing Bodies

Instrument of Government

The instrument of government is a legal document which sets out the procedures to be followed by governing bodies. It sets out the composition of the governing body and lays down rules about the number of governors required to form a quorum (enough members present to make decisions), who is eligible to serve as chair of the governing body, when governors must withdraw from a meeting, and when they cease to be eligible for membership.

Articles of Government

This articles of government set out the powers and duties of governing bodies. They cover the curriculum, staff appointments, pupil discipline, control of capitation and the annual report to parents.

Composition of Governing Bodies

Governors are made up of Parents, Local Education Authority (LEA) Officers, Head, Teacher and Co-opted members. The number for each representative depends on the size of the school.

Parent Governor

Any parent who has a child registered at the school can be a candidate in a parent governor election and vote. The term 'parent' also includes 'guardian'. Parent governors report to other parents on the governors' meetings unless material is confidential.

LEA Governors

LEA governors are appointed by the Council on the nomination of the political parties. They agree on how the places available on each governing body should be allocated between them.

The Head

The Head is automatically a governor unless s/he chooses not to be, in which case s/he is still entitled to attend meetings but without voting rights.

Teaching Governors

Any teacher employed permanently at the school can be a candidate in an election for teacher governor and vote. This applies to full-time and part-time teachers. Teacher governors are elected by the teaching staff on the school, but they are not delegates of the teaching staff and cannot be mandated. Their role is to give governors the benefit of their professional expertise and of their knowledge and experience as teachers in the school. When teacher governors report to staff on governors' meetings, they cannot discuss confidential material.

Co-opted Governors

The 1986 Education Act (1) empowers governing bodies to co-opt additional governors to serve as full members of these bodies. These governors are usually from the community. (*From the London Borough of Ealing handbook for governors, compiled for newly appointed governors*).

Chapter 8

OFSTED inspections and the centrality of Equality of Opportunity in raising standards

Rehana Minhas

The purpose of inspection is to identify strengths and weaknesses in schools so that they may improve the quality of education offered and raise the standards achieved by their pupils. (Introduction to the *Framework for Inspection* — OFSTED Handbook for the Inspection of Schools, Part 2)

It is not only the pupils and students who are subject to assessment. The school's members are regularly assessed, until recently by a team of Her Majesty's Inspectors (HMI) and, since 1992, by OFSTED. The role of OFSTED in a) maintaining school performance and b) upholding their own criteria for equal opportunities, will be influential in enabling (or otherwise) the achievement of black pupils. The Office for Standards in Education (OFSTED), a non-ministerial government department, came into existence in September, 1992. The Office is headed by Her Majesty's Chief Inspector (HMCI) of Schools for

England and members include HMI. OFSTED has new arrangements for school inspection under the Education (Schools) Act, 1992 and the implementation of its own programme of inspection.

The new system required all Inspectors to be registered after the successful completion of a two-stage training programme, provided or approved by HMCI. OFSTED also trained and assessed members of inspection teams. Lay Inspector training has been contracted out to accredited trainers. Each inspection team must have at least one lay member — that is, someone without previous paid experience of school management or the provision of education. OFSTED invites tenders for Inspections and awards contracts to teams of inspectors. Privatisation and market principles mean that cost is a factor when OFSTED considers bids from various teams, in the new four year cycle of Inspection. A number of inspections, with reports published, carried out using the *Framework* as part of the training under the supervision of HMI, are the subject of analysis in this chapter.

The Framework for Inspections and the related guidance are statutory — ie obligatory — for all inspections. The *Framework* includes the code of conduct for inspectors, inspection requirements, the inspection schedule which outlines the areas that the Inspection Report should include. Under the section: **Factors contributing to these findings**, Equality of Opportunity is clearly required as an important factor in raising educational standards.

Context

The acknowledgement given to Equal Opportunities within the *Framework for Inspections* and the Handbook becomes more significant when considered within the political and ideological context of Britain in the 1990s and the orientation of most of the education reforms of the 1980s and 90s (Searle, 1989; see Davies, *et al*, 1989). In the 1990s there is a marked increase in racial attacks, fascism, anti-semitism (Runnymede Trust, 1994), sexual harassment, and popularisation of homophobic attitudes. The continuing economic recession sees ever-increasing poverty (Amin, 1992). The events in Europe in the name of 'ethnic cleansing' have further encouraged populist nationalism. The climate in Europe helps to legitimate insular views about 'British Heritage' — a view which excludes and denies the existence, contribution, struggles and achievements of black and ethnic minority communities in Britain, allowing them no place in the historical or cultural picture. So there is cause for wonder at the way that OFSTED has helped to regain small but significant ground for Equal Opportunities.

In the first edition of the *Framework*, in August 1992, equality issues focused on institutional arrangements, individual practice and the outcome for pupils. When it was revised a year later, one wondered what would become of the section on Equal Opportunities — would it disappear? Would the intrinsic link between equality and standards be made explicit? It was a time of much lobbying and campaigning by educationists concerned about all pupils' entitlement. At a national conference in 1991, an officer of the NCC was confronted over the failure of the Council to publish the recommendations of the NCC's Working Party on Multicultural Education. The outcome was that the 115-strong conference gave a mandate to the Runnymede Trust to prepare and publish a document to provide schools with the missing guidance. *Equality Assurance in Schools: Equality, Identity, Society,* was launched by the Runnymede Trust in 1993. Its first principle was that without 'equality' there could be no 'quality' of education.

OFSTED's first *Framework for Inspection* (August 1992) had required that the arrangements for equality of opportunity be evaluated by 'the extent to which the particular needs of individual pupils and groups of pupils arising from gender, ability, ethnicity and social circumstance' are met within the teaching and the life of the school generally. Detailed areas were identified for examination, including policy statements for different aspects of equal opportunity; admission policies, intake and exclusions; pupil grouping arrangements; curriculum content and access; class management; resources; pastoral provision; and leavers' routes. Also to count as evidence was: 'the use made of support teachers and other provision under Section 11 of the Local Government Act 1966'.

The accompanying guidance in the *Handbook for the Inspections of Schools* further amplified the evaluation criteria for ensuring equality of opportunity, for example that: 'Indicators such as examination results and attendance rates are scrutinised for information on the performance of minority groups of pupils, including the most able.'

Under particular features, OFSTED recommended that policies and provision for under-fives should clearly indicate awareness of the particular needs of young pupils who are working in their second language. It also required Inspectors to be aware of the implications of legislation related to equal opportunities.

The revised OFSTED Framework and Guidance

The revised *Framework* of August 1993, strengthened the section on equality of opportunity overall and required that schools comply with the Sex Discrimination Act (1975) and the Race Relations Act (1976). Inspectors were now required, as part of their evidence, to consider:

a) standards of achievement of individuals and groups

b) assessment of pupils' needs within the curriculum, thus making explicit the link between equal opportunities and standards.

The guidance paper too, was much improved. In the August 1993 Handbook, guidance on Equal Opportunities was doubled to four pages. The core task is: 'to assess the influence of the schools practice and policies on pupils' access to the curriculum and their achievements'. It alerts Inspectors to the dangers of accepting subjective views about intake or the local community. The impact of a school's Equal Opportunities policy is to be judged by the extent to which it informs the school development plan and is reflected in the school documentation and departmental literature. Outcomes are to be monitored, and detailed attention is given to provision for bilingual pupils.

Inspectors need to establish whether the quality and quantity of curriculum support is adequate for bilingual and/or black pupils, travellers and pupils from refugee families; whether the needs of these pupils are reflected in school policies; whether Section 11 staff are enabled to plan in-class support effectively. The quality of provision for bilingual pupils is further emphasised in the section on evidence, where it is stated that the central issue should be the school's effectiveness in helping bilingual pupils gain access to the whole curriculum.

Under particular features, attention is again drawn to relevant legislation which refers to equal opportunities in education. The Children Act (1989), the Education Act (1981) and the Education Reform Act are cited. Citing the Education Reform Act as having a specific bearing on Equal Opportunities, brings pupils' entitlement to the centre stage. Inspection arrangements are now required to ensure that attention is paid to equal opportunities across the range of inspection tasks including the inspection of individual subjects. In particular school provision for English as a Second Language requires specialist inspection — the main references being in the sections dealing with literacy, spoken English, teaching, staffing, links with the community and/or the section on English as a subject.

A significant development is the acknowledgement of community languages. Letters inviting parents for a meeting with the OFSTED Registered

Inspector and the questionnaire for parents have been translated into eleven community languages: Bengali, Gujarati, Hindi, Panjabi, Urdu, Cantonese, Greek, Turkish, Vietnamese, Somali and Arabic. This came about in response to parents at a particular school making specific demands for letters to be translated, during a training OFSTED Inspection led by HMI in Haringey, and the translations are now available for all Inspectors.

There are some lapses, however. Rather than the 'examples' of reports in fictitious schools, included in the 1993 *Handbook,* it would have been more helpful to have cited genuine reports of schools that recognise equality of opportunity as central to high educational standards.

In the report of the imaginary 'St James', for example, a short paragraph (page 21 para 54) is included that focuses on gender. A report on 'Barchester School' devotes four paragraphs to the fact that this fictitious school has no equal opportunities policy, but this is not mentioned in the section on management nor on the quality or range of the curriculum.

It is worth noting that sections of the Heads' questionnaire make specific reference to ethnicity and gender in terms of profile of pupils, reference to Section 11, details of pupils whose main first language is not English. The sections on examination results and student destinations, however, require information in terms of gender but not ethnicity.

On paper, then, the 1993 document developed and extended OFSTED's concern to assess equality of opportunity in school inspections. The 1994 *Framework* provides no new guidance on equal opportunities, which means that the existing guidance stands.

The effectiveness of any guidance can only be assessed in terms of its impact on schools and the work of the Inspection team. From my personal observations of schools in the LEA I work in, the impact of the OFSTED criteria and requirements has been tremendously positive. The Handbook for Inspections is a weighty document, and it is necessary to draw particular attention to the centrality of Equal Opportunities to the Inspection process. Where this is done, however, the impact is considerable. Schools with Equal Opportunities policy statements and codes of practice have had an impetus to review their policies and structures for implementation. Others who had been 'diverted' from Equal Opportunities with the pressures of implementing the National Curriculum and assessment have to arrange for INSET days on Equal Opportunities. And the few schools who have yet to be convinced about the centrality of Equal Opportunities to educational provision and achievement, have been activated to address a range of pertinent equal opportunities issues.

OFSTED reports

Is it also possible to guage the impact of the Equal Opportunities documentation by looking at the Inspection reports by OFSTED trainees that resulted from the Stage Two Training Inspections led by HMI and also from key reports on education and raising standards that OFSTED has published.

LEA Advisers for Equal Opportunities analysed 71 OFSTED reports: 30 Primary, 36 Secondary, and five Special Schools, for their approach to Equal Opportunities. The reports were of schools with 10% or more pupils from black and ethnic minority communities. The analyses were conducted by former HMI.

Sharply revealed was the variation in approaches to Equal Opportunities. The key issues were the use of language and tone either to value the cultural and linguistic diversity of the pupil intake or at worst to problematise it and see it as contributing to low standards. In some reports very little or no reference was made to the pupils' cultural heritage, and the reference to equality of opportunity was very limited.

In the best reports, Equal Opportunities considerations appeared throughout: in the main findings, standards, pupils' spiritual, moral and cultural develop-ment, management planning, teaching and support staff, subject areas and detailed summaries of key issues under the specific section on Equal Oppor-tunities.

So there is significant variation in the awareness and expertise of the OFSTED teams and Registered Inspectors with regard to Equal Opportunities. The Runnymede Trust (1994a) analysis of the first fifty OFSTED reports bears this out. It is important that parents and governors ensure that the Evaluation Criteria and Guidance in the *Framework* and the *Handbook for Inspections* are applied to the fullest; i.e. that Inspectors' observations include documentary analysis and elicit evidence from discussions with pupils, staff and parents (see also page 84).

OFSTED Training

The expertise of black advisers and LEA inspectors committed to Equal Opportunities is of essential value and needs to be recognised by OFSTED and systematically tapped. The number of black and ethnic minority educationists invited to undergo training for OFSTED remains very small and raises concerns about the selection process and which applicants are prioritised for training. In their annual report, OFSTED record the number of applicants, the number who successfully complete the training and the number awaiting training. There is, however, no breakdown in terms of ethnicity. Furthermore, the five day training for OFSTED Inspectors does not include anything specifically in terms of assessed tasks on Equal Opportunities. If OFSTED is serious about its commitment to Equal Opportunities and if it wishes to increase its accountability to black parents, the training procedures need to take these matters into account.

The centrality of race, class and gender equality to educational achievement is well established and documented through years of research (see, *inter alia*, Centre for Contemporary Studies 1980; Coard, 1971, Milner 1975, Myers 1989, Swann 1985). The very fact that equal opportunities can be hindered through institutional arrangements and individual practices needs to be visibly treated as of serious concern. Standards in education cannot be improved unless quality and equality are addressed together.

Key studies by OFSTED

Two key reports published by OFSTED on raising educational standards invite comment about their stance on Equal Opportunities.

1) OFSTED — *The teaching and learning of reading and writing in reception classes and Year 1*. Spring 1993. This report is extremely problematic and serves to contradict the key principle in the Handbook for Inspectors that warns them against 'accepting subjective views about either the intake or the local community'. It is dismissive also of the core task of schools: effectively to help bilingual pupils gain access to the curriculum. The three references to bilingual pupils in the report cited in the main findings (para 7), Reading in Reception Classes (para 7) and Reading in Year 1 Classes (para 15) state that standards were low because the majority of pupils spoke English as a second language. The following statement is made in all three cases:

> In some classes where the standards were low, the quality of the teaching and learning was good. In these classes the majority of pupils were drawn from socially disadvantaged backgrounds or spoke English as a second language.

The report does not refer to the quality of provision for these bilingual pupils and makes no mention of Section 11 support. It also assumes that all the pupils have the same experience of English as a second language. It fails to exemplify strategies for teaching effective reading and developing oracy at a young age. Indeed, the report serves to legitimise low expectations of bilingual pupils.

2) The Report, *Access and Achievement in Urban Education*, on the other hand, is welcome. It summarises evidence from a survey conducted by OFSTED in seven urban areas of England characterised by high levels of social and economic disadvantage.

Minority ethnic groups were represented in three of the study areas: Slough 39%, Greenwich 24%, and Derby 15%, with substantial proportions where the primary and secondary schools on the survey were located in Slough and Greenwich. Some of the key findings of this report are noteworthy. For instance, under *Curriculum Achievement and Assessment* (page 14 para 12), we find 'Effective nursery programmes offered the social education essential for those children with little experience outside the family as well as providing a bridge to school'. And this: 'A nursery with a high proportion of pupils whose first language was not English planned work progressively using the expertise of a teacher of English as a Second Language and of a multilingual non-teaching assistant. In this case the gradual acquisition of a second language had the effect of focusing planning directly on pupils' needs'.

In the section on provision in the Primary Sector, there is this passage under *Curriculum and Teaching* (page 16 para 16):

> In the absence of accurate assessment teachers used more generalised estimates of pupils' abilities which led them in some schools to overestimate the effects of poverty and social disadvantage and to underestimate the potential ability of pupils. This was most marked in one school which had a high percentage of pupils of Asian background.

It continues in para 18: 'Too often teachers' low expectations resulted in depressed pupil achievement'.

On *Achievement and Assessment* (page 17 para 19), the Report observes that: 'Few teachers taught pupils to use context clues so that they had additional strategies for new words and learned to concentrate on meaning and become confident, self-correcting readers'. These Inspectors clearly recognise the vital strategy of using context clues to aid bilingual pupils in the early stages of acquiring English.

The report also comments on *Provision in the secondary sector*. Regarding Curriculum and Learning, it notes (page 23 para 32) that 'Many teachers lacked detailed knowledge of the range of ability in their classes and were insufficiently skilled in recognising the particular needs of boys and girls, of children of minority ethnic heritage or of the more able pupils'; and, in para 34:

> Children rarely received the kind of feedback on their work that helped them to know what or how to improve... The outcomes of assessment were not used to determine the nature of subsequent work and pupils had little opportunity to review their overall performance and progress with staff.

The report also considers provision for particular learning needs, observing, on p.30 para 46, that: 'A withdrawal group in one school inappropriately mixed children with learning difficulties and bilingual pupils whose learning needs were quite different'. It also notes about Resources that 'Constraints meant that in-class support, both for bilingual pupils and for pupils with learning difficulties was provided for only some lessons'.

The Appendices for the report show that money spent on books and equipment per pupil in 1990/91 for Shire counties averaged £43 for primary, £84 for secondary schools, whereas in Metropolitan schools, it is only £35 for primary and £68 for Secondary Schools.

The *Urban Schools* report highlights this injustice and points also to other fundamental issues concerning assessment in schools:

- Assessment arrangements in schools need to prioritise the diagnostic assessment, which they show to be largely displaced because of the demands of statutory end of key stage assessments.

- Educational standards cannot be raised only through inspection of individual schools on a four year cycle. A range of areas in the education debate have implications for assessment in multi-ethnic schools:

    1. Teacher education is the vital place for installing a perspective on equality and justice, and the limitations of school-based 'mentor' support suggest that it is unlikely to provide such a forum

    2. Cuts in LEA Advisory Support Staff are eroding the monitoring of policy implementation and INSET

    3. Cuts and changes in Section 11 funding (see *Multicultural Teaching* 12.1) are coming at a time when the needs are great and the expertise is available and operating for the access, assessment and achievement of bilingual and black learners. As Bob Garrett and Steve Cooke (1993) observe:

        > Most insidious of all will be the denial of equality of opportunity for families and their children making it more difficult for those who do not receive equal access to the curriculum to participate in society. That is to the detriment of us all, and it is racism by another name.

    4. Education in inner city areas continues to be deprived of resources through the impact of LMS and formula induced underfunding. Fur-

thermore, in the same week as the OFSTED report on *Access and Achievement in Urban Education* was published, new cuts that will affect inner cities were announced (Searle 1994). In the words of the *Observer's* education correspondent reporting that the Government is to strip millions of pounds from schools in deprived inner city areas (Oct 93) 'Local Authorities with a large proportion of single parent families and substantial ethnic minority populations will be the main loser', adding that 'affluent Shire counties will gain the most'.

The long-awaited OFSTED report on Section 11 funded projects published in 1994 argues strongly for future support for such work, targeting resources for minority ethnic pupils. However, the Single Regeneration Budget threatens less money and more competition for the little there is.

Conclusions

OFSTED Inspections are, as we have seen, capable of evaluating and therefore promoting educational opportunities for children and specifically for black children. But if inspectors skimp on the requirements of the OFSTED *Framework* and disregard the guidance, school inspections will fail to ensure equality and therefore fail to raise standards. Four yearly inspections are, in any event, less influential in determining the life chances of black pupils than is day to day assessment. And, as we have seen, other factors in the political/educational arena are also shaping children's educational chances.

To make progress, parents will have to use the mechanisms of OFSTED inspections, voicing their concerns if schools are not meeting their children's needs, and making specific demands for Equality of Opportunity and their children's statutory entitlement to education.

Antiracist teachers can also play a role, through their networks and also by using their expertise to produce specific guidance at all levels, building on the model of *Equality Assurance.*

More black educationalists need to go for OFSTED training and also to demand consistency in all reports regarding Equal Opportunities.

The Commission for Racial Equality should set up a dialogue with OFSTED about quality control with regard to the Equal Opportunities and should call for greater OFSTED accountability. As Caister's report for Haringey affirms:

• Campaigning for *real education* for enlightenment and liberation is ultimately the only way to ensure that black children and white, girls and boys, all gain their full entitlement to education and are accurately and constructively assessed.

- Equality of opportunity is a fundamental characteristic of the school — the aspects of school life which need to be addressed are listed: the language and content of the curriculum, teachers' and students' attitudes and expectations, the nature and distribution of resources, methods of assessment and the establishment of effective procedures for dealing with incidents of abuse. Finally, there is a commitment to create 'an environment in which diversity can flourish'.

References

OFSTED (1992) *The handbook for the Inspection of Schools.* August 1992

OFSTED (1993) *Revised Handbook for Inspection.* August 1993

OFSTED (1993) *The teaching and learning of reading and writing in reception classes and Year 1.* Spring 1993 (HMCI)

OFSTED — *'Standards and Quality in Education 1992-93'* Annual Report (HMCI)

OFSTED (1993) *Access and Achievement in Urban Education*

OFSTED (1993) *Hornsby School for Girls — Inspection Report*

Amin Kaushika (1992) *Poverty in Black and White, CPAG and Runnymede Trust*

Caister, Margaret (1993) Approaches to Equal Opportunities in recent OFSTED Reports' Seminar paper given at Haringey Professional Development Centre on 19 September 1993 (unpublished)

Coard, Bernard (1971) *How the West Indian child is made educationally sub-normal in the British school system.* New Beacon

Commission for Racial Equality (1987) *Enquiry into English Language Teaching in Calderdale.* CRE

Davies, Ann Marie, Holland, Judith and Minhas, Rhana (1989) *Equal Opportunities in the New ERA.* Tufnell Press

Garnett, Bob and Cook, Steve (1993) Perspectives on Section 11 in Leicestershire, *Multicultural Teaching* — Vol.12, No.1, Autumn

Richardson, Robin (1993) Section 11 funding — Troubled History, Present Campaigning, Possible Futures, *Multicultural Teaching.* Vol.12, No.1

Runnymede Trust (1994) *A very light sleeper', the persistence and dangers of antisemitism.*

Searle, Chris (1989) 'From Forster to Baker: the new Victorianism in Education' *Race and Class*

Searle, Chris (1994) Campaigning is education' *Race and Class.* March

Sivanandan, A. (1994) 'UK: Millwall and After': Racism and the BNP *Race and Class,* March 1994

TIZARD, Barbara *et al* (1989) *Young Children at School in the Inner City.*

Appendix 1
OFSTED (1993) Revised *Framework for the Inspection of Schools*

7.3 (ii) Equality of opportunity

Evaluation criteria

The school's arrangements for equality of opportunity are evaluated by the extent to which:

- all pupils, irrespective of gender, ability (including giftedness), ethnicity and social circumstance, have access to the curriculum and make the greatest progress possible;

- the school meets the requirements of the Sex Discrimination Act (1975) and the Race Relations Act (1976).

Evidence should include:

a. standards of achievement of individuals and groups;

b. assessment of pupils' needs within the curriculum;

c. the school's stated policy for equal opportunity;

d. admission policies, intake, exclusions;

e. curriculum content and access;

f. class organisation and management, teaching and differentiation;

g. the use made of support teachers, bilingual assistants and other provision under Section 11 of the Local Government Act 1966;

h. pupils' relationships.

The report should include evaluation of;

the school's policy and practice for equality of opportunity and the effects on the quality of learning and standards of achievement;

how well the policy is understood, implemented and monitored in terms of opportunities and support arrangements for individuals and different groups; where appropriate, a judgement about the use of provision under Section 11 of the Local Government Act 1966; and

any key points for action in relation to equality of opportunity.

Appendix 2
Draft Letter from the Appropriate Authority Notifying Parents of the Meeting For Parents

Name and Address of the Appropriate Authority

Dear Parent or Guardian

INSPECTION OF [SCHOOL NAME]

NOTICE OF MEETING FOR PARENTS, [TIME], [DATE], [VENUE]

As you may know, our school is shortly to be inspected as part of the programme of regular school inspections arranged by Her Majesty's Chief Inspector in accordance with the provisions of the Education (Schools) Act 1992. The inspection team will be led by [Name] (Registered Inspector).

An important part of the procedure is the meeting of parents with the Registered Inspector before the inspection. This meeting is held in order to hear your views of the school and the context in which it works to explain to you the inspectors' procedures. Naturally, before the inspection the inspectors will not be able to comment on parents' views, but they will take them into account in the inspection.

The Registered Inspector would be grateful if you would read the attached agenda and complete the parents' response form. Whether or not you will be attending the meeting, you are welcome to send you comments on the agenda items, or on any other issue, in writing before the meeting. The comments should be sent to:

(Name and business address of Registered Inspector/or name of Registered Inspector, c/o the school)

I hope you will be able to come to the meeting.

Yours faithfully

FOR THE APPROPRIATE AUTHORITY

Sayın Anne-Baba veya Veli,

TEFTİŞ EDİLECEK OKUL:

VELİLER TOPLANTISI İLANI: SAAT: _____ GÜN:

ADRES: .

Belki de bildiğiniz gibi okulumuz, Majestelerinin Baş Müfettişi (Her Majesty's Chief Inspector) tarafından, 1992 Eğitim (Okullar) Yasası (Education (Schools) Act 1992) uyarınca düzenlenen okullar teftiş programı kapsamında yakında teftiş edilecektir. Teftiş ekibinin başında Kayıtlı Müfettiş (Registered Inspector)

_____ bulunacaktır. Bu işlemin önemli bir bölümünü, teftişten önce Kayıtlı Müfettiş ile Veliler arasında yapılacak toplantı oluşturmaktadır. Bu toplantının amacı, okul ve okulun çalışma biçimi ile ilgili sizin görüşlerinizi dinlemek ve müfetişler tarafından yürütülecek işlemleri açıklamaktır. Doğal olarak müfetişler veliler tarafından getirilen görüşler konusunda teftişten önce herhangi bir yorum yapmayacaklar, ancak teftiş sırasında bunları göz önüne alacaklardır.

Kayıtlı Müfettiş, ekte gönderilen gündemi okumanızı ve veli yanıt formunu doldurmanızı rica etmektedir. Toplantıya katılacak olsanız da olmasanız da, gündem maddeleri veya başka herhangi bir konu ile ilgili görüşlerinizi toplantıdan önce yazılı olarak gönderebilirsiniz. Görüşlerinizi gönderceğiniz yer:

Toplantıya katılacağınızı umarız.

Saygılarımızla,

Chapter 9

Resources for raising achievement

Pat Keel

The main source of support for black pupils, and closely linked with their learning and achievement, has been Section 11 funding. We saw in Chapter 1 how the funding originated in a Local Government Act in 1966, contributing 75% of salary costs for staff who would be supporting the education of New Commonwealth pupils. In Chapter 3 we saw how it was assumed that new-comers to English might be rapidly assimilated into English language and culture by being put through an intensive programme of English language learning. This has been a tragic misconception which has persisted throughout the long saga of Section 11 funding.

The Early ESL model
The style of delivery of English as a second language was by what in linguistics is called the 'direct' method. This may be a highly convenient teaching methodology — the teacher transmits English language to the learner, without any reference to or account taken of the learner's first language. This method has enabled armies of English as a Foreign Language (EFL) teachers, some with no more than a few weeks' training, to staff the many institutions offering English language to would-be learners from overseas, or to acquire jobs teaching English in other countries.

English as a Second Language (ESL) teachers in the classroom have a different status. For a start, their target learners are settlers who require English for life in this country. The teachers might see themselves as having a role in imbuing their students with 'British culture' and this might become a salient teaching objective (Williams, 1967 in Gillborn, 1990). Secondly, in schools they have to be trained teachers but except for this, require no further specialist training. So in the early years of Section 11, teachers tended to drift into ESL work if they showed some aptitude for work with ethnic minority children. It often promised less demanding work with smaller groups of relatively manageable pupils, most of them Asian.

The other teaching method that shaped the early teaching of English to newcomers was 'immersion'. Pupils were withdrawn into separate units for what was meant to be an induction period, during which English language was the focus of teaching and learning. They had a diet of formal English, not always set within any immediate context. They were largely cut off from the curriculum in the mainstream classroom, away from the peers from whom they would have picked up more purposeful everyday language of school. The language units probably did not sufficiently build the confidence pupils need for successful social communication and for breaking their dependence on staff. When they did join the mainstream, sometimes after a couple of years in special units, they were frequently lagging behind in curriculum subjects, and this showed in their low achievement levels in the 70s.

A rethink of the 'withdrawal' system was needed. The case in Calderdale LEA, taken up by the Commission for Racial Equality in 1985 [CRE, 1987], highlighted the inequities and inadequacies of 'language units' away from the mainstream classroom. The Secretary of State agreed that such arrangements were unlawful and instructed the LEA to make more appropriate provision. Since then there has been a steady move away from withdrawal, especially since the Home Office disapproved. However present trends since the early 90s towards streaming and specialism, led by the National Curriculum and subject-based assessment, may herald a return to pre-Calderdale days [Dorn, 1992].

The isolation of pupils was not the only practice that required review. The teaching method used generally ignored the pupils' first languages and cultures. No deliberate use was made of the pupils' background knowledge and skills in their first language. Still less were these valued. Rather, they were seen as hindrances to assimilation. Pupils tended to become negative towards their home languages and cultures, instead of valuing them as part of their own knowledge base and identity, as we saw in Chapters 3, 5 and 6. They could feel out of phase with their parents, if they regarded them as lagging behind in adopting English language and culture (Taylor, 1981).

Bilingual model

Following the lead taken in ILEA from the late 1970s [e.g. by CUES, Bilingual Development/Community Languages Team, CLPE, English Centre, and Unified Language Service, etc] some schools gradually adopted more sensitive and positive approaches which place value on bilingualism. However, there were dangers in going too far with simply encouraging children to use their home languages in schools. In Tower Hamlets, for example, where there are large percentages of Sylheti speakers in the schools, it was observed that children did not always have sufficient opportunities to use English and make effective progress in learning it.

PLR assessment

The Primary Language Record (PLR), exemplifies a more balanced approach, reflected in some of the National Curriculum Guidance (quoted in Chapter 3). The Stages of English in the PLR were adopted by the Home Office for assessment of pupils' need for Section 11 support. Although the Stages of English were not intended as a basis for summative assessment but meant mainly to guide teachers in bilingual children's learning, they are nevertheless being used in schools to support LEAs' bids to the Home Office for funding. Unfortunately the National Curriculum Level Descriptions do not as yet incorporate allowances for language development for emerging bilinguals, as is reasonably described in the PLR Stages.

There is no central policy underlining the need to include bilingual development in the National Curriculum for children with bilingual potential. The result is that negativity to bilingualism is still evident in many schools. Pupils are reluctant to admit that they speak languages other than English at home, and staff may argue that they must defer to parents who want their children to learn and use English only. Parents, concerned primarily with their children's future job prospects, do not always recognise the value of their bilingual development, especially if they are not given confidence to do so by the school.

Section 11 administration

The administration of Section 11 has further contributed to its ineffectiveness. Originally LEAs applied for funding based on numbers of New Commonwealth children in schools. Because there were few checks on how funding was spent, LEAs and schools could use it for items which might have only the slightest connection with the educational welfare of ethnic minority children, and the fund was abused by schools concerned only to acquire 'another pair of hands'.

As such misuse increasingly came to light in the 1980s, the Home Office attempted to regulate the fund better, but the small number of Home Office department staff could not be expected to 'police' it. A review resulted in new regulations in 1990.

The fund became cash-limited and LEAs had to bid for a share, for projects lasting three or five years. They had to consult local New Commonwealth communities in defining their projects, and to show how consultation would continue throughout the project. In general, such involvement of the target communities themselves has been a plus. The bids have to be framed around a set of defined educational needs, and the strategies by which the needs would be met. Year-on-year targets and the means by which they would be monitored had to be stated and annual reports were required on progress towards targets. Staff responsible for work towards targets are named in quarterly financial statements, and the Home Office paid 75% of the salaries of these staff retrospectively.

Partnership teaching

The new Home Office guidance appeared to encourage LEAs and schools to focus more sharply on the essential purpose, ie to raise the educational achievement of the pupils concerned through providing language and learning support. There are now many schools where Section 11 support staff work successfully alongside mainstream teachers, providing the appropriate teaching and learning strategies for pupils to gain access to the curriculum, as well as the extra time needed for individual pupil attention. The Home Office has wanted projects to be effective in embedding suitable strategies within the mainstream curriculum through partnership teaching and INSET. Moreover, their guidance has shown recognition of the usefulness of bilingual support, thus encouraging the employment of bilingual teachers, instructors and classroom assistants. Information on employment is documented by the Local Authorities Race Relations Information Exchange. LARRIE is also a useful source of comparative data on LEA Section 11 projects (LARRIE, 1993, 1994).

The NFER Partnership Teaching Project [HMSO, 1991] has been influential in schools where it has been used, in promoting effective team planning and teaching between mainstream and support staff. Some excellent work has originated through the Project, which deserves to be widely disseminated and sustained. The Intercultural Education Project has grown out of the Partnership Project and is working to widen the use of partnership teaching, collaborative learning strategies as well as parental partnership.

Obviously the role for Section 11 teachers, both to support pupils new to English and to support mainstream teachers in using strategies to increase pupils' access to the curriculum, promises the most effective delivery of results. By these means all teachers would be providing language development across the curriculum to all pupils. However, in schools where senior staff are not accommodating of these strategies within the school development plan, or where there are not supportive language policies, any work of this kind can become patchy. A lack of resources also makes it difficult to allow enough time for team planning and teaching.

Training and status

Without INSET for staff at all levels appropriate strategies cannot be implemented. The squeeze on funds for training has meant that this particular area of professional development is usually neglected. Section 11 teachers tend, for the historical reasons described above, not to enjoy high status. Yet the demands of this work merit high status and its success depends upon it. INSET should be given higher priority if Section 11 teachers are to act as a specialist resource for mainstream teachers, who in turn need an understanding of how to incorporate this resource into curriculum planning. All too often Section 11 staff are still seen as merely the 'extra pair of hands', of whom the school may make general use, or as the person in charge of the ethnic minority pupils. Because they are now often regarded as LEA centrally pooled staff rather than as employees on the school's budget, they are likely to be poorly resourced for their INSET and teaching materials, the more so as LMS causes LEA finances progressively to shrink.

Recent administrative and financial pressures

Misuse of staff can still pass unnoticed because resources for monitoring are limited. LEAs, in any case, have been presented with an administrative nightmare. Without much guidance from the Home Office, each has had to work out their own systems for administration and monitoring — the required paper work is environmentally unfriendly to say the least! There have been annual data collections in respect of: ethnic monitoring of pupils, their progress on the Stages of English, their achievements in the National Curriculum and in GCSE and 'A' level examinations, as well as statistics relating to various other targets set, eg numbers of parents attending school meetings. The ethos of competing for funding from the Section 11 purse has meant that each LEA has had to keep complicated statistics and huge amounts of paperwork in its bids. Furthermore, the bidding system obliged LEAs to set very impressive targets! Some targets turned out to be unachievable. Despite LEAs jumping through these hoops the Home Office suddenly announced in November 1992 that it would be reducing its provision of 75% of salary costs to 57% in 1994/95, and thereafter possibly to 50%. In October 1993, Parliament was lobbied by a large delegation of Section 11 education staff from across the country. Ministers were asked to reconsider these cuts, which would severely weaken the effects of valuable work achieved by current projects. For the first time a concerted national campaign raised the profile of issues to do with the education of black minorities.

Single Regeneration Budget

However, soon after the lobby, the government announced that funding arrangements were to change still further. From April 1994 the Single Regeneration Budget (SRB), administered by the Department of the Environment, came into existence. The SRB takes under its wing some 20 programmes previously funded through different Departments, including the Home Office's Safer Cities, Section 11 Grants, Ethnic Minority Grant and Ethnic Minority Business Initiative. Local authorities in urban areas are expected to put forward composite bids addressing a range of inner-city needs. The projects must be seen to be promoting economic, industrial and social regeneration. They must incorporate partnership amongst public institutions, the private sector, voluntary organisations and communities. They should be income-generating and build in 'exit strategies' which allow funding to taper off as targets are achieved. Obviously, the underlying purpose of this government initiative is to significantly reduce government spending on inner-city priorities, and to draw in whatever private sector funds can be attracted into projects. EC funding sources are also being suggested.

It is dubious however, whether the SRB bidding framework can adequately accommodate educational needs — especially those of children in school. Their needs are not short-term and there cannot be quick financial returns to investors. There may be an official expectation that schools will absorb the cost of, and responsibility for, providing learning support for ethnic minority children. LEAs would then be under pressure from schools to devolve funding used for this provision, which is currently protected with 'mandatory exception' status, but for the DFE might remove this status whereupon LEAs will find it extremely difficult to fund coherent and consistent support across schools where it is needed.

Indeed these squeezes on funding raise many worrying questions about the nature of educational provision for ethnic minorities in the future. How will provision be consistent across local authorities? Will some be winners and some losers in this *ad hoc* securing of funds? Will the nature of provision depend on individual councils' bids and their fortunes in this lottery? In such a framework, how will the stability be achieved that is needed for work in education and educational provision be planned, organised and administered? And can the previous flaws in Section 11 provision be ironed out?

Race Issues

Some of the significant flaws in Section 11 *have* been removed. That the recipients of the fund should be only those of New Commonwealth background has been dropped. Since the 1960s there have been other non-New Commonwealth groups arriving in schools with similar learning support needs — Vietnamese and Somalis, for instance. Indeed their needs as pupils new to this country, perhaps traumatised by experience of war, can be even more challenging for schools (see Rutter, 1994). In 1993 parliament altered the original 1966 Act to include these new arrivals within the fund. This is helpful because treating them as a separate group has been divisive and impractable in schools.

However, there still remain core issues of race and ethnicity. We have seen in previous chapters how assumptions about the necessity to assimilate ethnic minorities into 'English language and culture' have underpinned the whole of education's response to the presence of black children. While the fund might have covered multicultural and antiracist education during the 80s, the new guidelines have reined it in closer to the original remit, that is, to provide pupils with access to learning through English language support.

Although the Home Office guidelines acknowledged that racial discrimination affects the lives of black minorities, they expect LEAs to resource multicultural or antiracist initiatives separately. Community language teaching too, can no longer be resourced through Section 11 funding. Yet bilingual support is recognised as valid —for the early years at least — and bilingual classroom assistance is supported. The messages seem ambiguous. It appears that there is a failure genuinely to endorse multilingual and culturally plural development, or to recognise how the educational welfare of black and bilingual pupils is inextricably tied to their having a learning environment free from racism in the classroom, and free from racial harassment in the playground and beyond. And although racism is undoubtedly a mainstream issue, staff whose specialist remit is the educational achievement of the children at the sharp end of it, must be able to adopt a holistic approach in their work. Perhaps local authorities will be freer to adopt such a holistic approach in future provision under the SRB — if their bid is successful!

Ethnic Monitoring

The ethnic monitoring upon which the dispensation of the fund has depended has caused further difficulties. Ethnic monitoring is vital in tracking the extent of racial discrimination in social and economic life, and broad black/white categories are acceptable for this. In the context of Section 11 in schools, ethnic monitoring is more detailed and increasingly divisive and problematic. In a modern world of travel, migration and inter-ethnic coexistence, it becomes more and more difficult for people to state their ethnicity definitively. Why should black people be constantly induced to fit themselves into categories? Already generations of British-born blacks or people of dual ethnicity, are uncomfortable with the narrow categories forced on them by ethnic monitoring. Effective and less contentious monitoring is an issue which should be considered in future arrangements.

Differentiating black groups from other minorities who also suffer discrimination and disadvantage in society, such as the Irish, and from others who fall into the social bracket of 'have-nots', is also problematic. For staff and resources to be seen to be provided for the particular benefit of black children is likely to increase resentment against them from those who have a limited awareness of the issues involved. This kind of difficulty is symptomatic of a system with fundamental inadequacies. 'Extra resourcing' is 'targeted' at the results of the inadequacies, instead of tackling their root causes.

Mainstreaming specialist provision

Many of the difficulties are a direct result of the singular manner in which language support is funded — out of not the Education budget but a Home Office purse. Should not extra funds be allocated to education, so that institutional initiatives for providing learning support to all pupils who need it can be co-ordinated and all be part of mainstream provision, albeit accommodating various specialisms? It is vital, for example, that learning support for black or bilingual children is treated as quite distinct from SEN support. There are nevertheless common principles and approaches towards dealing with disadvantage in education and there could be greater sharing and cross-fertilisation of strategies for providing learning support, whether for individuals or groups, for special or for mainstream curriculum development. There appears to be a trend towards this approach both at institutional and LEA levels. For this approach to work effectively, it needs to be sensitively handled. Teachers need time to collaborate, and they need supportive INSET and specialist staff to initiate and focus the work.

Although there is no question that all initial teacher education should be obliged to cover the main issues concerning black children's education adequately, meeting the educational needs of these children should be a specialist area, incorporating a bilingual approach. In order to strengthen this specialism there should be salary incentives for it, and better access for bilingual staff to pursue specialist courses. Unfortunately, discrimination against black staff is well documented [eg CRE, 1987, 1988, *Ealing's Dilemma* 1988]. The teaching profession poorly represents the country's population in ethnic composition — less than 5% are black and the percentage is falling. The paths to gaining recognition of overseas qualifications and being awarded Qualified Teacher Status [QTS] need to be clarified and made readily available.

There should be sufficient resourcing also for a network of regional specialist centres to develop appropriate teaching strategies and good quality materials, and for their co-ordinated dissemination to all schools. Unnecessary duplication could be avoided, and successful materials are worthy of quality production.

Finally, monitoring and evaluating delivery is essential. The framework for OFSTED inspections includes this area of provision (explained further in Chapter 8). Over the years ahead the efficacy of the process of OFSTED inspection will be tested, both in terms of raising the quality of education, and in terms of how well disadvantaged groups are supported in gaining their entitlements.

In the meantime, bearings could gainfully be taken by the government, LEAs and schools from evidence gathered in an OFSTED survey of educational provision funded under Section 11 (OFSTED, 1994 *Educational Support for Minority Ethnic Communities* [Ref: 130/94/NS]). The report confirmed the continuing need for this type of support and it found that the 1990 Home Office Guidelines have benefited provision. Partnership teaching, INSET for support as well as mainstream staff, the use of bilingual staff and promoting parental involvement are all strongly endorsed strategies. A whole-school approach to provision and integrated record-keeping, monitoring and evaluation, linked to the school development plan are all factors associated with effective practice. The report illustrates a successful LEA model on which a central project team manages projects in partnership with headteachers — a 'steering committee' clarifies targets and oversees administration. The central team acts in a 'monitoring and evaluating capacity' and as 'disseminator of best practice'.

It must be remembered that Section 11 provision was originally a temporary measure, a contingency fund intended to help assimilate New Commonwealth pupils. Dependence on the fund has extended over nearly three decades. That there is still a very real need for centrally provided specialist support for the education of black children is evident: i) black children are still subject to discrimination and still underachieving [evidenced eg. by Key Stage 1 SAT results], ii) the arrival of pupils new to English has continued (Rutter, 1994), and iii) with schools now managing their own budgets, it is unlikely that there will be a widespread hiring of specialist staff by schools for black children's needs. The onus clearly rests upon the government to ensure that there is an adequate contribution through education to building a society in which black minorities live on a par with their fellow citizens.

Chapter 10

Where to next?

Pat Keel

On balance this book may sound a despondent note, as each author has alerted us to causes for concern. Nevertheless there remain grounds for hope that we are approaching not a *cul de sac* but a crossroads, where fresh paths may be chosen. If indeed this turns out to be so, some attractive possibilities lie ahead.

For example, current dissent over National Curriculum assessment may lead to the central question — 'What is the essential purpose in assessing children?' — coming up for debate again. If we are able to agree, as was done at the time of the TGAT report, that assessment is a strategy vital to the processes of teaching and learning, then continuous diagnostic and formative assessment could become the more pertinent tools. Present over-emphasis on summative assessment represented by national tests at Key Stages may fall away. An acknowledgement that time, effort and resources must be focused on teacher assessment, would allow teachers to perform the essence of their job, ie fine-tuning each child's learning progression. Such fine-tuning requires their professional knowledge and skill, as well as effective school management structures which accommodate whole-school curriculum planning and organi-sation. Current debate and consultation by the government could lead to a reordering of these priorities in seeking better education for the nation's children.

Perhaps we would then be released from the current rigid standardisation of the National Curriculum and assessment, and free to open the path to genuine choices, involving all parties concerned — child, parent and teacher. The National Curriculum must offer a flexible framework for such choice, so that ultimately a teacher can provide motivation for, and facilitate each child's learning. Alongside this, parents must be kept in touch with their child's progress and enabled to provide informed support. Teachers understand that continuous assessment lies at the heart of each pupil's progression, in which they would want to keep the child and parents in partnership with them.

This partnership incorporates regular reporting to and consultation with parents, and should be the basis for much of the accountability expected from a school. Regular inspection is the other source of quality assurance and the drive towards better standards. There is no fundamental need for league tables, even if they could offer information of any value. They cannot in themselves ensure quality. Huge sums have been spent on glossily packaged tests, largely for the purpose of generating league tables. Those funds could have contributed substantially to raising the standard of our schools' learning environments and materials, or to the INSET teachers must have in taking up the challenges of the National Curriculum.

The Dearing Review did not face up to these issues squarely. It fudged (paras 3.34 — 3.43) the issue of how 'accountability to parents and society' can in fact be achieved through the application of 'short, well-conceived national tests in the core subjects at the end of each key stage', although the importance of continuous teacher assessment was admitted. The government's intention to insist on league tables continued to be signalled in statements like:

> At a national level, information about the achievement and the perfor-
> mance of schools is critical to the future well-being of the whole country.

If 'information about the achievement and the performance of schools' meant the range of information which might constitute value-added, then more of us would find this statement acceptable. However, the Report was very cautious over the issue of value-added by individual schools, although paras 9.16 -9.18 acknowledge that it requires investigation. A working group has been set up to:

> consider the extent to which any suggested measures might contribute
> useful information to parents, governors, teachers, headteachers and
> Government to complement the information from basic results from tests
> and teacher assessment.'

Dare we hope that a crossroads on the issue of value-added may be ahead? If we are to judge schools on the full range of indicators of both their educational delivery and their pupils' achievements, this is vital. Studies (Smith and Tomlinson, 1989; Goldstein, 1989) have identified several factors, including management patterns, in school effectiveness. Value-added is especially relevant for schools which tackle the task of delivery for numbers of children who face initial disadvantage. Perhaps Professor Michael Barber's study at Keele University, together with experience in LEAs such as Tower Hamlets (see Anne Sofer's letter to TES on 21 Jan 1994) will point the way towards national comparisons that are fairer than the discredited form of league tables witnessed recently. Factors such as reading levels at entry, social disadvantage, and English fluency will surely count in value-added assessment. The use of pupil and parental satisfaction as markers for school effectiveness is being flagged in the Keele study (TES, 25.3.1994). Interest in value-added is evidently growing, as the NFER is picking up a study begun in 1990 by the late Desmond Nuttall at the University of London Institute of Education [TES, 13. 5. 1994]. Several urban LEAs will contribute to this study.

Another central question not addressed by Dearing is *what* we should be assessing. Again TGAT indicated a broad area for assessment of achievement, reflected in the importance they placed on RoAs. Yet a spotlight has been thrown by the government on what is assumed to be 'basics' — or reading, writing, numeracy and science in their narrowest sense. Dearing has left us with these as core areas for Key Stage assessment. The 'breadth and balance' of the National Curriculum may now be jeopardised. The importance of other areas of the curriculum like Geography, History, Music, Art, PE is being stripped away. Teachers have been sceptical of the advice emerging from the curriculum advisory groups which SCAA hastily constituted to review the Orders for each subject. Like many government quangos, membership of the groups was hand-picked to ensure government policy is not overturned. The new 'slim-lined' curriculum may seem less demanding for teachers and pupils, but has this reduction been driven again by the wrong priorities — ie to reduce coverage for national tests whose main purpose is informing league-tables? Is 'entitlement' to 'breadth and balance' in the curriculum being sacrificed?

The indications from SCAA are gloomy, judging by their rejection of the the advisory group's special mention of the needs of bilingual children in the new English Curriculum Order. Chapters 3 and 5 of this book both demonstrate the inadequacies of earlier National Curriculum guidance statements regarding bilingual children. But these statements are at least an acknowledgement of these children as a group deserving special attention, and they offer the basis

113

for developing positive approaches towards them. However, there is increasing disquiet from national bodies such as the CRE, NUT and NATE (TES 15.4.1994) over the English Orders. SCAA's swim against a tide of opinion favouring a broader vision of English and language development may turn out to be short-lived.

We think that the debate over what should constitute language development will persist: whether it should be a programme limited to the narrowest interpretation of 'Standard English' or one with elements on a wider spectrum embracing the many varieties that exist today as well as other languages relevant in the lives of our pupils. Should we not begin by focusing children's interest and curiosity on the languages and English varieties they bring with them, using these to help them to gain a firm grasp of the processes of language? Standard English can then become part of a broad repertoire, along with home languages. This approach has been advocated by many educationists over the last decade at least (Cox, LINC Project, Language Literacy Unit, English Centre, CLPE). The clash with right-wing 'ministerial obsession' on this issue (TES, 13. 6. 1994) will provoke continued controversy. The switch in mid-1994 to a new Education Secretary who has teaching experience, raises hopes of more sense in future Government decisions.

Moreover, setting up the curriculum advisory groups may have opened a Pandora's box, setting loose debate and protest, probably for the best in the long run. Many teachers and parents will surely argue for a renewed emphasis on breath and balance in the curriculum. If, alongside this, the concept of value-added becomes practicably interpretable, assessment should be obliged to cover a wider range of children's potential achievement. Whereupon records of achievement will at last be able to take on their full significance for each child.

As yet there has been little development of the cross-curricular dimensions, which have the potential to breathe life and meaning into an otherwise drily academic and patchy curriculum. The necessity for all children to have a broad field in which to develop and achieve in knowledge and skills is well under-stood by educationists. In this book we have argued for the importance of this for black children and developing bilinguals, but a system that assesses and rewards achievement in a confined field will reduce all children's life chances ultimately.

We may be approaching a watershed also on provision for under-fives. Celia Burgess-Macey brings home in Chapter 4 the crucial part assessment plays at the first stage of a child's schooling. The approaches taken in assessment in the early years lay important foundations for the child's later development. In the early 1990s nursery education has acquired new political attention, possibly as an election issue. The report of the National Commission on Education [1993], drew public sympathy in calling for high quality nursery education for all children. Research is showing that a good start in the early years pays large social and economic dividends. The Commission argued that spending on this provision would be offset eventually against the costs of treating the various social ills such expenditure would abort. If in the next few years we do go down the path of universal under- fives' provision, a major source of unequal starting chances, often borne disproportionately by black children, would be removed. The issues raised in Chapter 4 about assessment in the early years would become even more significant.

Schools have been offered incentives to attract them to grant-maintained status, but most are choosing to remain with local authorities. Perhaps this is because schools are largely satisfied with the degree of autonomy offered under LMS and see little advantage in going independent. Some at least do not trust the political motives underlying the push towards grant-maintained status. Meanwhile, local authorities are busy building new relationships with schools, who in turn may be finding that their LEAs are best able to provide friendly, expert and cost-efficient services after all. If this proves to to be true, local authorities who are relied on to advise schools on their legal responsibilities could continue to encourage them to adopt a range of policies and practices covering ethnic monitoring and antiracist/multicultural approaches to the curriculum, which help to ensure compliance with equal opportunities legislation. As we have argued here, all children stand to benefit from such policy and practice.

The inter-relationship between quality of delivery and equality appears to be inherent in the OFSTED framework for inspections, although as Rehana Minhas has suggested, OFSTED's consistency in this matter could be strengthened. This is an aspect in which the role of certain national bodies could be increasingly influential over the next few years. The CRE together with bodies such as the Runneymede Trust and the Refugee Council, which monitor race issues, have a function in strengthening race relations legislation by bringing about better enforcement of the law, as well as drawing attention to where the law needs extension. It seems likely, judging from the Dewsbury example, that cases of discrimination on grounds of race and religion are set to haunt us in the coming years. But it is worthwhile, for the sake of long term interests, to face up to challenging scenarios where discrimination might otherwise flourish.

On a parallel front, teachers' unions and organisations such as NATE and NALDIC show encouraging signs of actively campaigning on equality issues in the curriculum, eg on supporting linguistic diversity. However, campaigns expressing the rhetoric of equality need to be strengthened with the hard evidence of research. Some of this is available in the data gathered through ethnic monitoring exercises carried out by the CRE and others. Teachers have a significant role to play in action-researching and disseminating their experience of curriculum development approaches which successfully enhance black pupils' access to the National Curriculum and assessment.

In the hurly-burly of getting the curriculum and assessment 'right', we must also keep track of how our pupils are changing. We are decades away from the time when most black children were new arrivals to this country. Now over half are British-born, and their experience is largely of this country. A growing number have parents of more than one ethnic or racial background, often part white (Alibhai and Montague, 1992). The culturally diverse nature of many children's lives — the particular richness as well as the tensions — is something that does not receive much attention. Too often in our education debates children are inadequately seen and almost never heard.

Finally, we have expressed a fundamental distaste over the current emphasis placed on the mechanics of competition. However, if it is possible to have fairer indicators to work with and by which to be judged, we may become better at evaluating which factors make schools effective in delivering quality education for each child. We are confident that if this were achieved the curriculum and assessment needs of black children will be central. And with that properly in place, all children can be assured of a high quality education.

Bibliography

Amin, Kaushika (1992) *Poverty in Black and White*. London, Child Poverty Action Group and Runnymede Trust

Athey, Chris (1990) *Extending Thought in Young Children*. Paul Chapman

Barrs, Myra (1990) *Words not Numbers*. NATE/NAEA

Blenkin, G. and Kelly (1988) *Early Childhood Education: a developmental curriculum*. Paul Chapman

Bolton, Eric (1992) 'Vision of Chaos'. In *Times Educational Supplement,* 31.7.1992.

Bourne, Jill (1994) *Thinking through Primary Practice*. Routledge

Bourne, Jenny, Bridges, Lee and Searle, Chris (1994) *Outcast England: how schools exclude black children*. London, Institute of Race Relations

Brice-Heath, S (1983) *Ways with Words: language, life and work in communities and classrooms*. Cambridge University Press

Brooking, Catherine Foster, Marina and Smith, Stephen (1987) *Teaching for Equality; educational resources on race on gender*. London, Runnymede Trust

Brown, Colin (1984) *Black and White Britain; the Third PSI Survey* Heinemann

Bullock Report (1975) *Language for Life*. HMSO

Carter, Trevor (1986) *Shattering Illusions: West Indians in British Politics*. Lawrence and Wishart

Centre for Contemporary Cultural Studies (1982) *The Empire Strikes Back*. Hutchinson

Centre for Language in Primary Education (1989) *Primary Learning Record*. London, CLPE

Clarricoates, C (1980) 'The importance of being Ernest, Emma, Tom, Jane. In Deem, R. *Schooling for Women's Work*. Routledge and Kegan Paul

Coard, Bernard (1971) *How the West Indian Child is made Educationally Sub-normal in the British School System*. New Beacon

Commission for Racial Equality (1987) *Inquiry into English Language Teaching in Calderdale*. London, CRE

Commission for Racial Equality (1988) *Ethnic Minority School Teachers*. CRE

Commission for Racial Equality (1991) *Lessons of the Law.* CRE

Cox, Brian (1990) *An English Curriculum for the 1990s.* Hodder and Stoughton

Craft, Alma and Klein, Gillian (1986) *Agenda for Multicultural Teaching* York: Longman

Cummings, Jim (1981) *Bilingualism and Minority Language Children.* Ontario Institute for Studies in Education, Canada

Davies, Ann-Marie, Holland, Janet and Minhas, Rehana (1989) *Equal Opportunities in the New ERA.* Tufnell Press

Department of Education and Science (1985) *Better Schools.* HMSO

Dorn, Andrew (1992) *School admissions and racial segregation.* ISSUES, Autumn

Dhondy, Farrukh et.al. (1982) *The Black Explosion in British Schools.* Race Today Publications

Donaldson, Margaret (1978) *Children's Minds.* Collins Fontana

Drummond, Mary Jane (1994) Scales of Injustice. In *Language Matters* 1993/4. London,CLPE

Ealing, London Borough (1988 *Ealing's Dilemma.* Ealing LEA

Early Years Curriculum Group (1989) *The Early Years Curriculum and the National Curriculum.* Trentham Books

Early Years Curriculum Group (1992) *First Things First; educating young children.* Oldham, Madeline Lindley

Edwards, Viv (1984) 'Language policy in multicultural Britain'. In Edwards, Viv (ed) *Linguistic Minorities, Policies and Pluralism.* London, Academic Press

Edwards, Viv (1986) *Language in a Black Community.* London, Academic Press

Eggleston, John (1988) The new Education Bill and assessment — some implications for black children. *Multicultural Teaching* 4.1.

Eggleston, John et.al. (1986) *Education for Some.* Stoke on Trent: Trentham Books

File, Nigel and Power, Chris (1981) *Black Settlers in Britain 1555-1958.* Heinemann Educational

Fryer, Peter (1984) *Staying Power.* Pluto Press

Garnett, Bob and Steve Cook (1993) Perspectives on Section 11 in Leicestershire, *Multicultural Teaching* 12.1

Gillborn, David (1990) *'Race', Ethnicity and Education.* Unwin Hyman

Gill, Dawn and Levidov, Les, eds. (1987) *Anti-racist Science Teaching.* Free Association Books

Gipps, Caroline (1990) *Assessment: a Teacher's Guide to the Issues.* Hodder and Stoughton

Goldstein, Harvey (1990) *Assessment in Schools; an alternative framework.* London, Institute of Education

Goldstein, H. and Nuttall, D (1989) *Screen Test for Progress.* Education Guardian, 4.7.1989

Gravelle, Maggie (1990) Assessment and bilingual pupils. *Multicultural Teaching.*9.1.

Great Britain (1990) *Section 11 of the Local Government Act 1966: Grant Administration, guidelines and instructions* (Annexe B). Home Office

Gregory Eve and Kelly, Clare (1994) 'Bilingualism and Assessment'. In Bourne *op.cit*

Grosjean, F (1982) *Life with two Languages: an introduction to Bilingualism.* Harvard University Press

Hamers, J.V. and Blanc, M.H.A (1989) *Bilinguality and Bilingualism.* Cambridge University Press

Hargreaves, A. and Reynolds, D (1989) *'Decomprehensivisation' in their Education Policies: Controversies and Critiques.* Falmer Press

Hargreaves, David H (1983) *Improving Secondary Schools.* London, ILEA

Hasbudak, Zeynep and Simon, Brian (1982) *Zeynep, that really happened to me.* London, ALTARF

Hester, Hilary (1984) Peer interaction in learning English as a second language. *Theory into Practice*, XIII, 3

Hester, Hilary (1993) *Primary Learning Record Handbook.* London, Centre for Language in Primary Education

Hillcole Group (1991) *Changing the future; Redprint for Education.* Tufnell Press

Home Office (1990) *Section 11 Administration: Policy and Guidelines.* Home Office

Jones, Crispin and Street-Porter, Rosalind (1983) Antiracist teaching and teacher education. *Multicultural Teaching* 1.3

Jones, Steve (1993) *The Reith Lectures.* BBC Radio 4.

Keel, Pat (1990) Section XI; towards successful bidding. *Multicultural Teaching* 9.1

Keel, Pat (1993) Section 11 -- support or sop? *Multicultural Teaching,* 12.1

Kennedy, C (1989) *Language Planning and English Language Teaching.* Prentice Hall International

Khan, Verity Saifullah (1980) 'The mother-tongue of linguistic minorities in multicultural England. *Journal of Multicultural and Multilingual Development,* 1.1

Klein, Gillian (1984) *Resources for Multicultural Education.* York, Longman for Schools Council

Klein, Gillian (1985) *Reading into Racism.* Routledge

Klein, Gillian (1993) *Education Towards Race Equality.* Cassell

Labov, (1969) 'The logic of non-standard English. In Atlatis, J (ed) *School of Languages and Linguistics Monograph Series no. 22.* Washington, Georgtown University Press

Leung, C. and Drury, R (1991) *English as a second language. Bilingualism and Languages Network, 1,3.* London, Centre for Educational Studies, King's College

Linguistic Minorities Project (1985) *The Other Languages of England.* Routledge and Kegan Paul

Local Authorities Race Relations Information Exchange (1993) *Section 11 Survey Part One.* London, LARRIE

Local Authorities Race Relations Information Exchange (1994) *Section 11 Survey Part Two.* London, LARRIE

Mac an Ghaill, Mauchin (1988) *Young, Gifted and Black.* Open University Press

Macdonald, Ian et.al. (1989) *Murder in the Playground; the Burnage report.* London, Longsight Press

Marland, Michael (1985) 'Some unspeakable truths'. *Education Guardian,* 18.6.85

Maxwell, Marina (1968) *Violence in the Toilets.* Race Today, 1.5

Milner, David (1975) *Children and Race.* Harmondsworth, Penguin

Moore, David (1980) *Multicultural Britain.* Save the Children

119

National Curriculum Council (1990) *English: Non-statutory Guidance and Programmes of Study*. DFE

National Curriculum Council (1991) *Circular 11: Linguistic Diversity and the National Curriculum*. NCC

National Foundation for Education Research/DES (1991) *Partnership Teaching*. HMSO

Nutbrown, Cathy (1994) *Threads of Thinking*. Paul Chapman

OFSTED (1992) *Handbook for the Inspection of Schools*. HMCI

OFSTED (1993) *Access and Achievement in Urban Education*. HMCI

OFSTED (1993) *Horsby School for Girls*. HMCI

OFSTED (1993) *Revised Handbook for Inspection*. HMCI

OFSTED (1993) *Standards and Quality in Education1992-3; Annual Report*. HMCI

OFSTED (1993) *The Teaching and Learning of Reading and Writing in Reception Classes*. HMCI

Rees O.A (1984) 'Education, language and ethnic groups in Britain'. In Verma, G.K. and Bagley, C (eds). In *Race Relations and Cultural Differences*. St Martin's Press

Rees, O.A. and Fitzpatrick, B (1981) *Mother-tongue and English Teaching to Young Asian Children in Bradford*. University of Bradford and Bradford College

Richardson, Robin (1993) Section 11 Funding — troubled history, present campaigning, possible futures. *Multicultural Teaching*, 12.1

Rist, Ray (1970) Student social class and teacher expectation; the self-fulfilling prophecy in ghetto education. *Harvard Educational Review*, 40.3

Robinson, B (1985) 'Bilingualism and mother-tongue maintenance in Britain'. In Brumfit, C.J. et.al. (eds) *English as a Second Language in the United Kingdom*. Oxford, Pergamon

Rose, Steven et.al.(1984) *Not in our Genes*. Harmondsworth, Penguin

Rosenthal, R. and Jacobson, W. (1968) *Pygmalion in the Classroom; teachers' expectations and pupils' intellectual development*. New York, Holt, Reinhart and Winston

Runnymede Trust (1993) *Equality Assurance in Schools; quality, identity, society*. Trentham Books

Runnymede Trust (1994a) *The First Fifty: a study of the first 50 Inspection Reports*. Runnymede Trust

Runnymede Trust (1994b) *'A Very Light Sleeper'; the persistence and dangers of antisemitism*. Runnymede Trust

Rushdie, Salman (1982) The New Empire in Britain. *New Society* 9 December.

Russell, A., Black, P., Bell, J. and Daniels, S. (1990) *Assessment Matters no. 8: Observations in school science*. SEAC

Rutter, Jill (1994) *Refugee Children in Schools*. Trentham Books

Scarman Report (1981) *The Brixton Disorders*. HMSO

Searle, Chris (1989) *From Forster to Baker: the new Victorianism in education*. Race and Class. June

Searle, Chris (1994) Campaigning is Education. *Race and Class*. March

Shipman, Martin (1990) *In Search of Learning*. Oxford, Blackwell

Sivanandan, A (1994) UK, Millwall and After: Racism and the BNP. *Race and Class*, March

Skutnabb-Kangas. T. and Toukomaa, P (1976) *Teaching Mogrant children's Mother-tongue and Learning the Language of the Host Country in the context of the the Socio-cultural Situation of the Mogrant Family*. Research Report for UNESCO. Tampere, University of Tampere

Smith, David and Tomlinson, Sally (1989) *The School Effect*. Policy Studies Institute

Spencer, Sarah (ed) (1994) *Immigration as an Economic Asset*. IPPR and Trentham Books

Stenhouse, Lawrence et.al.(1982) *Teaching about Race Relations; Problems and effects*. Routledge and Kegan Paul

Stierer, B., et.al. (1993) *Profiling, Recording and Observing; a resource pack for the Early Years*. Routledge

Stone, Maureen (1981) *The Education of the Black Child in Britain*. Collins Fontana

Stubbs, M (1990) 'A statement on Bilingualism' in Redbridge High School English Department Handbook

Sutton, Ruth (1992) *Assessment; a Framework for Teachers*. Routledge

Swann Report (1985) *Education for All*. HMSO

Taylor, Monica J (1981) *Caught Between; a review of research into the education of pupils of West Indian origin*. Windsor, NFER/Nelson

Tizard, Barbara et.al. (1988) *Young Children at School in the Inner City*

Tomlinson, Sally (1980) The educational performance of ethnic minority children. *New Community*, 8.3.

Tomlinson, Sally (1990) *Multicultural Education in White Schools*. Batsford

Tosi, Arturo (1982) 'Between the mother's dialect and English'. In Davies, A (ed) *Language and Learning at Home and School*. Heinemann Educational

Troyna, Barry and Ball, Wendy (1985) *Views from the Chalk Face*. Coventry, University of Warwick

Troyna, Barry and Hatcher, Richard (1992) *Racism in Children's Lives*. Routledge

Troyna, Barry and Williams, Jenny (1986) *Racism, Education and the State*. Beckenham, Croom Helm

Twitchin, John (1988) *The Black and White Media Book*. Stoke on Trent, Trentham Books

Wardhaugh (1986) *Languages in Competition*. Oxford, Blackwell

Whitehead, Marion (1994) 'Why not happiness?. In Gammage, Philip and Meighan, Janet (eds) *Early Childhood Education: taking stock*. Education Now Books

Wiles, Sylvaine (1985) Learning a second language. In G.Wells (ed) *Perspectives on Language and Learning*. Lewes, Falmer

Williams, Jenny (1979)' The Younger Generation'. In Rex., J and Moore,R. (eds) *Race, Community and Conflict*. Oxford University Press

Wilson, Amrit (1978) *Finding a Voice; Asian Women in Britain*. Virago

Wolfendale, Sheila (1993) *Baseline Assessment; a review of current practice, issues and strategies for effective implementation*. An OMEP UK Report. Trentham Books

Wright, Cecile (1986) Ethnographic study. In Eggleston *et.al.*(1986) op.cit.

122

Index